SNIPPETS

OR

HOW I SURVIVED THE VIETNAM WAR

A KILLER CAT

A GRENADE IN MY LUGGAGE AND

OTHER GOOFBALL ADVENTURES

BY

CHUCK TWEED

It was a dark and stormy night: Overused.

I was born at an early age: Ditto.

I always wanted to write a book until I discovered…

. . . I HAVE THE MIND SPAN OF A GNAT.

Or, as my adoptive Dad Bill sometimes jokingly told me: "If your brains were gasoline, you wouldn't have enough to start a Pissant's motor scooter." He was a country boy. What can I say?

The skies parted, Angels sang, the sun shone through on St. Anthony's Hospital in Oklahoma City on August 14, 1944, and Charles Neal Warfield, Jr. was born at 8:34 a.m..

What an eclectic man Charles Warfield (My biological father) was for the following reasons:

1. My mother found out he was married to someone else while married to her.

2. He had several children (some we may not know about), and he wanted the males to be named Charles, after him. Upon finding out this news in my later years, I decided that if I were to hold a convention of his many sons named Charles, we would have to rent out the Staple Center! (FYI: I was the first Junior in the bunch. Big whoop!)

I just realized that my sister Susan (Charlie also suggested "Penny")may not be the only Susan. Will have to suggest a bigger venue.

---

3. He had a photographic memory. Something he did not pass on. I did get his bald gene. Lucky me. His sister told the following:

A. He picked her up one evening and gave her a stunning cocktail dress, while he was dressed in some sort of military uniform. Odd, since he was not in the military at the time. She was all of 17. She was seated on a couch between two women. The woman to her right was "beautiful" and "very friendly." They were having a pleasant chat when Charlie walked up and said he was sorry he had not introduced them. "Sis, this is Esther Williams."

At the party, a small group of men got to talking about a tiny restaurant in Italy to which they had been. Charlie soon entered the conversation and added the name of another bistro down the street. His sister sat dumbfounded. He gave the name and address and how it looked inside and out. After they left, she asked him about the conversation about Italy since he had never been there, and he replied he had read a book the night before.

B. He picked his sister up one day and took her to a small airfield and asked if she would like to go up in a plane with him. Her instant reply was no and told him she never knew he was taking flying lessons. He smiled and said he had read a book last night. She watched him fly the plane for a few minutes and land.

* * * * * * * * * * * * * * * * * * *

Faye Garten gave me my life. She was my 9th grade drama teacher at Jarman Junior High (where I would later teach) in Midwest City, OK. I knew that I wanted to be a drama teacher like her. Almost off to a rocky start. I played the father in a one-act play. During the show the class laughed, especially at me, which did not sit well as I was giving the dramatic performance of my life.

I sat down and thought I smelled smoke coming out of my ears. The guy in front of me turned with a big smile. "You were so funny. That was a really funny comedy." What? Comedy?? I was hooked. At the end of the year Mrs. Garten said she had some good news and bad news. She would no longer be teaching at Jarman. What the heck did we care, we were going to Midwest City High. Then she added she would be going to Midwest City High. The skies parted, Angels sang. Oh, wait, already used that one.

It was one happy day for many of us. She taught us everything we needed to know. I mean everything. When I got to college, I found myself breezing through the drama program. (The same cannot be said of the science department or the math department or the...But that's another story).

Five minutes up on that subject for now.

* * * * * * * * * * * * * * * * * * *

Millions can identify with going off to college/university/ wherever. To have that freedom. (Insert evil grin) However, much time was spent at the theatre either being in a play or working on scenery. At the time it was called Central State College, then Central State University to the present University of Central Oklahoma. One of my greatest honors was working on the yearbook staff. Dear friend Dorothy Forbes (Harris) was editor, and I was on the writing staff. As it was the 75th anniversary of the school, she wanted to put the school coat-of-arms in the book.

Imagine our surprise to find out there was no coat-of-arms. Four of us created and submitted a coat of arms, which was approved by President Garland Godfred. The fun part is the Latin at the bottom: Ubi Motus Est, which means 'Where Movement Is.' Although maybe a little boring sounding, that was the closest we could come to what was then a hot TV show, 'Where the Action Is.'

Dare I say, I don't think one student on campus now knows that. You're welcome! The emblem is on everything now. A former student came to visit me wearing a sweatshirt with the logo, which I had not seen before. I asked him to buy me one which I would pay for, stating I had helped design it. He laughed and pointed to the bottom of the shirt with the founding date...1890. He bought me one anyway. I still have it, 35 years later.

* * * * * * * * * * * * * * * * * *

Confession: I am the luckiest man because when I was teaching I met the most amazing students. To this day I am friends with many of them and proud of what they have become. Grady Lee Richmond was one of the nicest students ever. Kind to everyone and liked by everyone. He called me one day from LA and said he was going to be in a series (after many commercials, TV spots, and stage acting) called "The Ranch." Earlier, he had had a small part on "Two and a Half Men," and Ashton Kutcher told him he was funny after the taping.

When I asked Grady who was in the series, he immediately said, "Ashton."

"Who else?" I asked. After a few seconds, he said the man playing the dad was...uh....Sam Elliott. Knees buckled at this, the room started to spin. "And, uh, the woman playing the wife...Oh, what is her name? "Oh, yeah, Debra Winger." THE Debra Winger??

My immediate response was, "Remember, you were nothing until I met you and was your mentor. I taught you everything. I want to fly out and watch a taping and meet them." Yes, I really said those exact words.

During the taping while I sat in the VIP section (folding chairs behind the set with a monitor to watch, and I loved it). Sam came up and we stood. "Who is this?" he asked.

Grady smiled, "My old drama teacher." He stammered, "I didn't' mean *old* old."

Sam and I shook hands, and he put his hand on my shoulder, and smiled. "You don't look old enough to be his old drama teacher."

After the show I got pictures with both Sam, (who, when he poses, puts his arm around your shoulder, pulls you in and tilts his head down), and Debra. She noted her husband had done theatre in Wichita, and I said I had friends there. She was delightful. Afterwards, Grady asked me what we talked about. He said bigwigs were there that night and the cast was to mingle, and she was with me for like 5 minutes (of sheer ecstasy).

I have the pictures on my phone and will show them to anyone at the drop of a hat. When I got back to the hotel, a friend sent me a text asking did I know Sam's birthday was August 9, 1944 and mine was the 14th? His year was 1944 and my year was 1962. Wait a minute, that was the year I graduated from high school, but that's another story. Oh, it gets better: Mila Kunis, Ashton's wife, was born August 14, 1983. Am I in good company or what?

* * * * * * * * * * * * * * * * *

Baby snippet: My mother told me when I was a baby I had a wide bottom and white, white hair, which when photographed, made me look bald. Like I am today. Full circle. There is a picture of my sister and myself sitting together. I look like a triangle with the baby blubber butt in a diaper, going up to my white/bald head. Because she thought it was funny, my sister liked to push me over, because I could not get back up. She thought it was funny in spite of mother telling her not to push over her baby brother (one year younger). The story goes she could not pronounce Charles but came out with Buddy. (Don't ask), and that nickname followed me through my freshman year in college. To this day old old friends (Thanks, Grady) either call me Buddy or Bud. Once I heard what she had done and called me Buddy, I called her a Bi...

Moving on.

* * * * * * * * * * * * * * * * * *

My cousin Linda is the best travel companion ever. For 19 years we traveled to Paris, London, Austria, Bora Bora, Russia, Casablanca and Spain (to name a few). Snips from those travels:

1. Standing in Red Square in Russia, of all places, and a couple with a little girl (Five years old maybe) came to us and asked if we would take a picture of them and their daughter they had just adopted from Mongolia. She had blonde hair, adorable, spoke no English and was obviously very shy. I took the camera and squatted down and showed her how to give me a high five. She looked at her mother, who gave approval, and we both giggled with a high five. As I gave the camera back I asked where they were originally from (get ready for

it)...Norman, Oklahoma. Add old adage here: Small world.

PS: Same thing happened in Saigon (more on the war later) as six of us were walking down a street and saw four other soldiers. Small chat and Bingo. One of them was from Oklahoma City. As we separated for maybe 10 steps, he and I turned at the same time and said, "Small world."

Remember this was a long time ago, so Linda and I never felt threatened when travelling. Even in Russia where the police walked the streets with AK47's. In my mind I kept thinking I looked soooo much like a tourist, therefore no threat. Apparently worked.

We took "The Sound of Music" tour (in Austria, of course). So many people know that movie line-for-line. The actual front of Captain von Trapp's villa is not the back as seen in the movie. They are two different places. Ah, the movies. The organization who bought the premises had to move the gazebo because people kept climbing over the wall for pictures. The tour went to the park where it was located. Although they were working on the arena where the concert took place at the end of the movie, they let us come in. Takes your breath away. No matter they did not escape like that in real life, but took a train out. It was almost overwhelming seeing the movie play in my head. I had to smile as I faced the stage and looked up to my left to see the side of a hotel.

When we began our descent into Vienna, guess what? It's flat. Hell, might as well be back in Oklahoma. (Strike that last sentence). We landed and were immediately shuffled to a two-prop plane, with one of the big blades outside the window. Must confess, I really kept my eye on the blade to be sure it did was it was supposed to do.

And, just like the movie, as we approached Saltzburg, there was one bump on the landscape, then another, and the hills were suddenly alive with....

I don't drink coffee, but when we stopped at a sidewalk café in Casablanca, I ordered one. Tasted really strong, but okay. Knock me down and call me Shorty, but as we were approaching our next stop to eat lunch, I felt sick, stomach churning. I got in the lobby and excused myself and went outside some feet from the establishment, looked around to see no one, and quite promptly decorated a small tree with vomit. I swear, the trajectory of the spew looked like something out of "The Exorcist." I took a picture to remind me of the event and the tragic tree. No vomit appeared in the picture and no people or pets were involved in the event. I'd be glad to show the picture on my phone.

Pass? Okay.

The morning we left Paris, a cold weather snap came, and you could see your breath. We had no coats but bought sweatshirts. We left Paris for St. Louis, where my cousin lives, and I continued on to Oklahoma City. As we were about to land the pilot said, "Well, folks, it's still hot in Oklahoma City, It's 97 degrees at 10:00 p.m." Picture my lungs collapsing as I walked out of the terminal.

I will snippet this later, but I was Production Director of the Jewel Box Theatre in Oklahoma City when the Murrah Building was bombed. That was April 19, 1995. In June, Linda and I were on a tour bus in London. The guide asked everyone where they were from. As we were in the front seats, she and I were asked first. As we know, not everyone is quiet with people softly chatting about this, that, and the other. Linda said, "St. Louis," and I said, "Oklahoma City." Suddenly, the bus was dead silent. When we got off, 12 people came up to me and said they were sorry. I was confused until one said the bombing in Oklahoma City was just horrific, and they wanted me to know they were thinking of everyone. Most touching, I thought. I did not tell them the actual extent of my involvement. Next time the town/state naming went like this: Linda: "I'm from St. Louis." Chuck: "Me, too."

* * * * * * * * * * * * * * * * * * *

My sister was a police officer, as well as her husband. I got to ride with her on a few night shifts. The first stop on my first night was a domestic dispute (hated by most officers because of how it can go right or horribly wrong. As I write this, a second police officer has died after being shot during a domestic dispute).

We were on a property in the middle of nowhere. A lone house sat there, with not much lighting inside or out. It was deathly quiet. As Sis got out, she said, "No matter what happens, do not get out of the car." As I slid down, she approached the front door. Eventually, and thankfully, it all turned out okay, but that was the longest 40 minutes, ever.

 My mother rode more often with her, and told me Sis stopped a drunk driver and put him in the caged back seat while she looked in his car for evidence. He leaned forward and tapped the divider and slurred, "What did they get you for, honey, prostitution?" Mother told him who she was, and he started begging her not to say anything. She agreed. However, my sister, when told, was fit to be tied and said she would have beat his ass had she known. We laughed about that event for years.

* * * * * * * * * * * * * * * * * * *

I am horrible at math. My dad could do it in his head. In college, my mother worked in our bank. On one occasion, well maybe two, okay, three tops, she called me to tell me I was overdrawn, which prompted my standard answer, "Well, fix it."

My first year of teaching, I was directing a play at school and my half-brother stopped by. In he walked: tall, blonde, blue eyes, football player at Midwest City High School, as well as a terrific baseball player. (At a little league baseball camp, instead of usually pitching, they put him on third base. Afterwards, my dad asked why and was told he was the only one who could throw to first base without it bouncing). So, there he stood, and I took a break so I could chat with him. In the middle of our chat, one of my girls walked up and batted her eyes.

"And who is this?" she purred. I told her it was my brother, and, without batting an eye, she looked at me and asked, "What happened to you?" My brother and I laughed. She burst into tears and hugged me, saying she was sorry. Brother left and it took a few minutes to calm her down. She apologized for days to come.

Somewhere I have a picture of our house around 1946. Between the two pillars by the front door hangs a hand-painted sign on a sheet: "Quarantine." It was me. A little girl a few houses down was playing with a cat, and I joined her. She got diphtheria and I caught it from her. Mother told me one night she heard me gasping and ran in and reached down my throat and pulled out a big string of phlegm, saving my life. I was not told until later the little girl had died. Sidebar: In college at a party there was a palm reader. Not a big believer, I avoided her all night. Toward the end as we prepared to leave she told me she had not read my palm. Of course, everyone chanted for me to do it. Why did I care as I was not a believer?

Imagine my surprise when she told me I had had a disease as a young child, and almost died. She also blurted out that I loved sex. Can you believe it? But that IS another story with no snippets on all the fun times I had when....

On my driver's license it says I have green eyes, but many people think they are blue.

On an early trip to New York, a friend and I took the ferry to the Statue of Liberty. Most people were at the back, looking at the skyline. There were two kids at the front. I told them their mother wanted them and they ran off. I stood at the front, grabbed the rail and broke into song: "Don't tell me not to live, just sit and putter," from "Funny Girl," as we had just seen it. My friend laughed. I asked her what was so funny? She pointed to the captain at the window behind us. He smiled, gave me a thumbs up and tooted the horn.

* * * * * * * * * * * * * * * * * * *

I mentioned earlier, when I was traveling, about being asked where we were from on the bus. I was both a teacher at Carl Albert High School, but also Production Director of the Jewel Box Theatre at the First Christian Church: A church with a huge white dome, four floors with classrooms, a large kitchen, and on the North end, the theatre.

April 19, 1995, was opening night. There have only been two times I have been home really sick when two major events happened: The Twin Towers and the Alfred P. Murrah Building bombing. I woke up and at 8:55 a.m., went to the couch and sat down and turned on the TV. At 9:02 a.m. I heard a boom. I thought nothing of it as I lived very close to Tinker Air Force Base, and we hear them all the time. I felt worse and went back to bed.

Around 10:30 a.m. someone called and asked what I was doing. Sick, I said. Turn on the T.V., it's very important. I staggered in, turned on the TV and saw the unfolding catastrophe. Like many people, my mind just exploded, not knowing what was going on. Calls started coming in from the church, friends, the actors in the play. Would the show go on? Will you cancel the run? I knew I had to get to the theatre.

The first thing was to cancel opening night. The leading lady called me to say she could not come in, anyway. She was the spokeswoman for the OSBI (Oklahoma State Bureau of Investigation) in Oklahoma City and would need to do press conferences, etc. My Box Officer Manager came in, and we called the audience to tell them there would be no show.

The authorities needed to set up a temporary headquarters, and the church offered their space. Suddenly, it was inundated with frantic people looking for information about friends and loved ones, or family victims, and the press, both local media coverage and national stations.

The floors were prioritized by need. The first floor was used for people checking in for any news, filling out papers, and waiting. The top floor, guarded, was for cases that were beyond grief. Eventually, the national guard had to be called in as people kept trying to sneak in. One famous person flew in and tried to bribe a fireman to let him use his uniform so he could get in. He didn't. We soon had tags so we could walk around and help as needed.

While a reporter was in the lobby, live on air, a ruckus broke out behind her. An officer grabbed a young man when he began fighting. Someone grabbed my arm. It was a friend who begged me to help, as it was her brother, distraught over a missing aunt. Over I went and walked out with them. We eventually got him to calm down enough to get in the police car.

I cancelled the first weekend. I have never felt such grief. People would see my tag and stop me to chat. Lots of tears. Lots of love. Lots of loss.

Anytime you saw the Red Cross on air for updates, it was in the Jewel Box. Oprah Winfrey, we heard, had flown in to talk with Pastor Don Alexander. We never saw her, nor the interview on air, since for the first two weeks, it was 24/7 local coverage.

I cancelled the second weekend and re-scheduled patrons for the remaining two weekends.

I would always talk to the 6-8 national guards outside the theatre when I came in from teaching school. One day my parking spot by the theatre was taken by a local news station van. The reporter, noted to be aggressive (in my opinion), stepped out of the large truck. I asked her politely to please move as it was my parking space. She glared at me and said she would not.

I ambled over to the guards. "We are so bored, Chuck," they lamented.

"Want something to do?" I grinned. Of course, they jumped at the chance. I told them my reporter story, and all of them went to the van. I stood on the porch and watched them talk to her while the reporter glared at me. And moved.

At the end of the third week, most of the activity was over. A few people remained to help anyone who happened to show up.

Years later another half-brother came to visit and asked to see the Bombing Museum. My sister had been there. I had not. He was surprised. I told him I did not need to see it, as I had lived it. Perhaps corny, but very true. I have not been back.

On the anniversary a few years back, they showed clips on local TV. Among the many scenes, the camera in the lobby of the church showed me helping someone. Come to find out, of the 168 deaths, two were people I knew. A former student, Karen Gist, an absolute delight, and Rheta Long, who was a volunteer at the theatre. At the last performance, director Martha Knott said she wanted to introduce me to a very good friend of hers. Turned out he was the principal leader who coordinated everything at the church during those first weeks. He had said he had not been out since the event, but Martha said the comedy would do him good. Afterwards, he thanked me for the laughs. Laughter can be a great help in such times. Took me a long time to not think about it so much.

I was Production Director for 41 years and made so many friends. It was just a perfect time. Actor Ed Harris, a student at the University of Oklahoma, was cast as King Arthur in "Camelot." He tells the story of coming out for a curtain call opening night and watching the entire audience standing, applauding, and cheering. He says he has never felt anything like it before or since. I was supposed to be one of the three knights but was too busy with school and other projects. Darn it, we could have been best friends. He was most gracious to later send an autographed picture to use in our program.

* * * * * * * * * * * * * * * * * *

My brother had a membership at a gym and got a complimentary pass, which I gladly accepted. DAY ONE: MBE, or Muscle Bound Employee, greeted me. I was 128 pounds, and we looked like a before-and-after ad in the floor to ceiling mirrors. He said we could start with leg lifts. On my back, he lowered the bar on my feet and said to do no more than six, or something low, and went to help others. I thought, this is not too bad, I'll do a few more. As fate would have it, on like the 12th leg lift, the bar came down, but my legs could not push it back up, but only wobble from the strain.

I grunted and groaned, but to no avail. I just lay there. Over came MBE who lifted it up. When I awoke the next day, no lie, I was like a board. I could not (for real) move. I slid out of bed onto the floor. Getting in the car to go to school was painful. I never confessed to my students what happened, but they helped me around all day, and it took four of them to maneuver this rigor-mortis-of-a-teacher gently into my car and watch the board drive away. DAY TWO: Not!

* * * * * * * * * * * * * * * * * * * *

Vietnam Nam: Nice place to visit, but I would not want to live there. First of all, I told them I could not go when they told me I had to go, because I was getting an early out for college, and it would only be there for six months. Apparently, they were not amused. Big Surprise. I went.

But first, I went to Ft. Bliss, Texas for basic training. Upon arrival SSgt Smith (Louis Gossett, Jr. before there was a Louis Gossett, Jr.) called our platoon out to begin to show us the basics of standing at attention, right and left face, about face, and marching. We saw the other men looking at us from their balconies and windows, wishing they were us. Made us proud. And we made sure he was always proud of us.

One time, skinny PFC Tweed (no first names) had to crawl under barbed wire in mud, without ringing a bell. I got to the end to see a pair of boots. I stood up and there stood a SSgt from another platoon. He bellowed (why always bellowing?), "I think you just rang a bell, Private."

Stupidly, I answered I had not. SSgt Smith approached, asking what happened. After hearing the bellow brat, SSgt Smith looked me in the eyes and said, "Tell me what happened, and I will support you." I said I would go back, and did, and still did not ring the #@& bell.

Some fun facts: I had never fired a weapon before, but loved it and even got a Marksman medal. Skinny boy could run. All I had to do in those heavy combat boots was to lean forward and off I would go. As I approached the last lap in a race, I was behind one runner, when SSgt Smith stepped out and yelled at me, "Move your skinny ass, Private." Boy, did I ever. And won.

In training we had to use pugil sticks where you have two big, padded balls at each end, and you prepare to beat the living socks off one another. I mean, some of those future soldiers really went to town on each other. I told some guys standing next to me that we should bend over and pant like we had just finished, and did a demonstration. As they laughed, up came a sergeant who looked at me, "I see you've already fought." He sent in the guy next to me.

We respected SSgt Smith and were always winning events because we didn't want to let him down. And all of this with very little yelling. Over the years I have thought of him and actually wished skinny PFC Tweed (no first names) had called or written to him to tell him how he impacted my life. You might want to consider doing the same to a mentor.

When we got our orders, I heard, "Tweed, you are going to Washington." Boy, oh Boy. Me going to Washington DC to hobnob with very important people. Might become a general if I work really hard. Very impressive, Washington, DC, no? It was Washington state, which took me to Ft. Lewis, Washington and lots of fun until the Viet Nam shock.

My bunk was closest to the back door and the latrine. One morning I woke up and felt something furry by my foot. Note: when you sleep in a bunk, you slide in because it is so tight you could bounce a quarter off it, and it saved time so you did not have to make your bunk every morning. As I whispered to my bunk mate and a few in nearby bunks, they saw a small lump. What to do? Nothing. They stood there watching to see if I would be eaten alive and taken to another planet, or stayed there for weeks waiting for it to come out.

A movement. Another. Up the critter slowly wiggled. The herd that was very close, bent over looking at the lump, now took four giant steps backward. Closer. Closer. A tiny black nose appeared. Then two eyes as out popped a puppy. I have no idea how he got down there without waking me. Right on cue, the sergeant bellowed, "Has anyone seen my puppy? He got out of my room last night."

Several of us were always together at Ft. Lewis, Washington. So when Schaffer invited me to a card game at his tiny, tiny house in nearby Steilacoom, I agreed. As we entered, I noticed the other two I came with looking around. I saw nothing. "Where is he?" one asked.

"Somewhere around," was the answer. I was then told the story of this cat, as big as a cougar, that Schaffer took in...sort of. The cat came and went, but...BUT, he was a terror and many times attacked guests as well as his nemesis. About 15 minutes into our card game, we heard a low growl. All eyes went to "Kennedy halves" as they tightened up and had heads pinwheeling as they looked around.

The cat/cougar peeked around the corner. You could hear a pin drop until the beast let out a slow growl and, in a crouched position, slowly moved toward his prey: Us! Suddenly, I felt a hand grab me and jerk me up on the table. What a sight: four grown men standing on a table, shaking like frightened little kids. Slowly he came. We froze.

Suddenly, he lunged for the table and Schaffer batted at his extended claws at least five times. Schaffer jumped off the table, beast swatting away, claws out, foam at his mouth with beady red eyes, (Cancel the last two), and grabbed a big broom. He opened the trap door to the basement, and the bitter foes went at it for what seemed like a long time, until the beast went down the stairs. The trap door slammed shut and was locked tight.

As we big babies sat down, I had to ask, "Does this happen often?" as I wiggled in my chair to be sure my underwear was still clean. Schaffer's reply: "Yep." Three days later the cat/cougar/beast left and never came back. Probably to join a witches cult or something. But, by then, Schaffer had bought a barrel to make beer, which exploded at 3:30 a.m. one morning.

But that's another story.

When I was in the sixth-grade mother sent me to 'The Little Store" as it was called and close to our house. I gave the cashier a ten dollar bill and she gave me change for twenty. Out I walked with my treasure. I got home and showed mother the change and told her how I was going to spend it. Next thing I knew I was sent back to return it. Mother told me the cashier would have had to put her own money in to cover it. When she thanked me and told me about having to pay for it herself, I said, "My mother made me." (Rotten Kid)

If you look at my fingernails you will find them clean. I never worked on a car in my life. Actually, to sidetrack, I did a commercial for an oil company, and was to put a can of oil in the car. Empty can, of course. I was looking for where the hole might be. Up walked a man dressed in farmer jeans and asked what I was doing. After I told him, we both were looking for the hole. A third man came up and we three stooges looked in vain. A woman in her 40s walked up and asked what we were doing. She laughed, pushed us out the way, pointed where to put in the oil and smiled. "It's my car." But I digress.

Back to Viet Nam. I am told that the soldier who did maintenance on the company jeep had been moved, and I would take over. ME? The first day I drove the jeep to the area where they all went for maintenance, if needed. Up went the hood. I looked left and then right to other drivers moving this, checking that. What to do? What to do? The only thing I could think of was...to dust it. The right and left came over. "What in the hell are you doing to that jeep?" "Dusting." They were always nice enough to me, but we never performed surgery on it. Anyway...

I was standing in line in some office, where if you get out of line you lose your place. A Vietnamese man came in excitedly, looked at me and yelled, "You jeep on fire."

Big laugh. I was not about to get out of line. That is, until an American soldier came in yelling at me that my jeep was on fire. It turned out to be minor, and that was the last day I ever saw the dust-free motor. You could eat off of it, that's how clean it was. I mean it. It was that clean. Shiny. Clean. Perfect. (Note to self: Stop the exaggeration).

We've all heard you have to laugh to keep from crying. A friend and I were talking about COVID and how there was a toilet paper shortage. "You know why, don't you?" She enlightened me. "One person sneezes and ten people shit in their pants".

Maestro Joel Levine had conducted me at Lyric Theatre, and asked me to be part of the first Yuletide Festival at the Civic Center with the Oklahoma City Philharmonic, the Canterbury Choir, and the OCU dancers under director and friend, Jo Rowen. I adore Joel. He is so giving, kind, funny and talented. He gave me a tape from the Chicago production he had just conducted. I was to do "The Night Before Christmas" with music to be underscored by the Philharmonic.

I watched the Chicago version on tape and thought I could manage it, although I don't read music. Took the music tape home, and for the life of me, could not get it to match what I was saying. Depressed, on Monday I told them I was quitting because, try as I might, I could not get in sync with the music. I started to leave, and Joel asked me to wait. He came out after a few minutes, smiling. "Well, no wonder you could not match the music. It was recorded backwards." I got the corrected tape.

All the recent news about guns on sets reminded me of when we did a play at the Jewel Box that required an actor to grab a gun and shoot upstage at the end of act one. We were a theatre in-the-round. The actor was to shoot the blank gun, and the director, behind the set, would reach up and pull out a pin so the picture dropped to the floor, showing a pre-drilled gunshot hole.

The shot was fired, and the director (behind the set) felt a pain under his right arm. He looked to see red running down the side of his white shirt. He had been shot by a real bullet. The ambulance pulled up at the back door and very quietly loaded the director and took him to the hospital. At intermission, a little old lady pulled the stage manager aside and whispered, "I just want to say it was a little noisy at the end of act one." She was guaranteed it would not happen again. As the director was being rolled into surgery, a news reporter called him for an update. It even made a tiny blurb in the New York Times. Somehow, the gun was not properly checked, and the real bullets were left in instead of props being inserted. That random shot could have been catastrophic. There are theatre gods!

Some people who get gifts can be so ungrateful. Take the time my sister found some of my grandmother's checks and took one. She filled it out in her 8-year-old handwriting, and off we went to the drugstore and bought them all gifts, and maybe one or two items for us. Ye gods and little fishes, you would think we had robbed a bank in a shootout. Our parents told us it was a crime, and the police might come to talk to us, or worse. My sister and I had to sit at the dining room table for hours. Finally, dad told us to go to bed and get some sleep. Like that would happen.

Some idiot high school guy caught my sister and me (She got me in more trouble!) because she had taken two cigarettes from my mother's purse and we went to the grade school we attended close to our house, and rocked the teeter-totter, being so cool as we smoked.

The stranger saw us, grabbed us, took us home (we were so scared we told him where we lived) and reported the crime to my parents. Imagine our surprise when they told us they did not mind if we smoked, but they would prefer us to have our first real smoke with them.

"But, Buddy," Dad smiled, "real men smoke cigars." Like he did. Susy got the cigarette, and I got the cigar. I'm only guessing, but I think my face went through at least 6 different color changes as I "smoked." Fast exit to the bathroom for a you-know-what. Never did that again. My sister was not so fortunate and died from COPD at 69 years of age after a long three-year battle. Sad to lose your best friend.

The first helicopter in which I was supposed to ride in Vietnam started to ascend. But it tilted, and a blade took a chunk out of the pavement. We all got out. When told to return, I said no. A few threats, but no action, and off they went. When I did ride in one, as we were flying over low brush, I could see some young Vietnamese men running around. I leaned out and yelled Hello and waved. I was jerked back in. "You Idiot, those are Viet Cong who could shoot up here. Stay inside".

Auto-Rotation. A word that still today makes my rear end pucker. While in yet another helicopter ride amidst all the noise, I thought I heard my name and the words "Auto-Rotation." The captain flying was over my work section. Over the Saigon River, suddenly it became very quiet. The helicopter had apparently malfunctioned and shut off, and we were all going to die as we plunged toward the Saigon River.

I heard "Auto-Rotation," my name, and a snicker from the captain. I undid my seat belt and prepared to jump into the Saigon River. It was quickly becoming bigger and bigger. I was pulled back in and told they thought it might be funny to perform an Auto-Rotation, where in practice, the copter is turned off, and a recruit pilot must restart it. Except there was no recruit on board, just two experienced pilots. For several days after, the captain would pass me, smile and whisper out of the side of his mouth, "Auto-Rotation." I can't confirm it, but it was reported that where I had been sitting, there was a hole in the seat. Apparently, as I plummeted toward the river, my ass bit a hole in it. I was not charged with any war crime.

One of the saddest pictures in Vietnam was mail call, when soldiers would stand in rain or shine hoping for a letter, package, anything, and receive nothing. Heartbreaking when mail call was over, and we started back to the barracks, and there they stood, head down, shoulders slumped. I will forever have that image in my mind. Good ole Mom wrote every day. Maybe just a paragraph, but at least something. My then-wife was also a good writer. I still remember hearing yelling and crying when someone received a 'Dear John" letter. Mother sent an actual box of homemade chocolate chip cookies. I think I got a small bite of one.

School and I, as you might have guessed by now, did not get along well. Let's start with kindergarten. The first day, after 30 minutes, I stood up and informed the teacher I did not like school and was going home. I turned to the door. She ran after me, followed by the entire class. I was told I ran around the school building. Imagine driving by seeing a kindergarten kid running, followed by the teacher, followed by the entire class. After very strong encouragement from my parents, I went back. Gag!

College. Up late for rehearsal. Did not read the story for homework. The professor said in the story, the character had the great American disease. He asked someone for the answer. Remember, we are talking the 60s, so I thought it must be cancer. Ironically, the student he asked said the same thing. The class erupted into laughter that went on for a long time. What else could it be? "I see you did not read the story, because the great American disease was...traveling".

Lordy, lordy. I thought about not including this tidbit of my war stories, but here it goes. Picture it. The base in Saigon was AMMC (Air Material Management Center) with a concrete water duct next to it, and on the other side of that, Vietnamese families living in a few houses we could see into. Behind that was a field with something growing. I tell people that one afternoon I was standing and heard a whiz go by my head.

It was a bullet! I fell over and everyone around me started falling for protection, running for cover with jeeps and security swarming all over. Told that story many times and not once was I asked where I was. However, it finally happened. I was asked. I said it was so scary and I heard it whiz by. Where were you? I was just trembling I was so scared. Where were you? I sucked in my breath. I was actually on the diving board at the pool. Took the wind out my sails for that heroic war story. But, it did happen.

Bora Bora is, as expected, stunningly beautiful. Linda and I got an over the water bungalow. There was a small section of the floor in the living room with glass so you could see fish swim. Turn on the light at night and it was so peaceful. We booked a dinner and Polynesian show. A dancer had a ball on a chain that was on fire around his ankle. He swung the ball as he jumped over it. Suddenly, it came loose, aimed right for Linda's feet, which she quickly pulled up while the audience gasped and screamed. He ran over and profusely apologized. It was the same hotel the Kardashians stayed in when they visited. I saw it while channel surfing. However, they were in a somewhat larger, bigger, more luxurious, expensive (feel free to add more adjectives) than we.

Another tour to a small part of an island where we had lunch and swam with baby sharks and sting rays. We had our picture taken with a man in waist-high water holding a sting ray and kissing it. Note to all men: It was winter for them in June, so the water was cold, and I would have been a spectacular soprano.

Landed in Paris, rented a car and drove to Ax-En-Province. We had lunch before going to the hotel. I love, love how they take time to eat and enjoy each other's company. No rush. My stomach thinks my throat has been cut if I don't eat by 6:00 p.m. at the latest. Had to laugh one night as we were eating dinner at 9:00 p.m.. Heaven!! I don't drink wine, but if it's really sweet, I love it. So, we had a couple of glasses for lunch at a café and were feeling pretty good. I remembered the name of the wine so I could order it at the resort for dinner. The young man came over to take our order. He did not speak English well. I pointed to the name I had remembered for the wine and told him I wanted a glass. He looked confused. I repeated my order. He put up a finger to halt the conversation and went to the bar. An English-speaking gentleman came over and asked me to repeat my order, which I did. He looked where I was pointing and informed me, with a smile, that I had just tried to order a glass of fish to drink. Note to self: Put on bucket list to learn a foreign language.

I saw Raul Julia as "Dracula" on Broadway. At the end of act two, the Count visits Lucy in her bedroom. She is swooning on her fainting couch when Dracula puts one knee on the edge, rips open his shirt and bends down for the bite. Just before he connects the lights go out.

Suddenly I heard approximately 200 women in the audience have an orgasm in the dark.

Fast forward when I directed the show at the Jewel Box. Playing Dracula was Ray Nicholas, a former student, football player, and black-haired hunk. Just like New York, Ray ripped open his shirt on opening night to show a smooth, muscled chest, and bent down, and as the lights faded, we heard a swoon from an older lady who sighed out loud, "I wish I was 30 years younger." Giggles and applause followed.

After the show she asked me if I was the director. I confirmed I was. She asked if she could meet Dracula. I got Ray, who came out to say hello. She was giggling and blushing like a teenager. "Could I," she stammered, "touch your chest?" Ray looked at me, and I shrugged. He said yes, and she put her hand on the center of his T-shirt for a few seconds, thanked him and walked out the door.

Sad note. The woman playing Lucy was in an abusive relationship with her husband. It got so bad that she told a friend she was moving out and to come get her the next afternoon. She took a nap while waiting. Her husband doused her with gasoline and lit her on fire. At the hospital, I was told, she took the arm of a nurse walking by, and told her that her husband had done this. And she died.

Yet another time I did "Dracula," Bill Hart designed a bat with red eyes and soft rubber wings. It was to be let loose backstage, and swing up to the center of the theatre in-the-round. Standing off stage at a door was Bill, who would reel the bat to him on a fishing line. As fate would have it, Bill had to be out of town for two Saturday performances. I would do the bat flying.

Practiced. Ready to go. Showtime. Bat goes to the center, where it proceeds to get stuck and swing back and forth as I watch the audience's heads bounce back and forth in unison, as if listening to an upbeat song. I gave a jerk on the wire to release the friggin' bat. It started down the line as I reeled in it. To my horror the bat left the line and dropped into a man's lap on the first row, who promptly screamed and threw it up in the air. The row behind him dove out of their chairs.

Second Saturday looms. I practice. Bat cooperates. Showtime. Same thing. But this time the bat crashes at the bottom of the stairs as I furiously try and reel him in. The bat turns on its back and does the back stroke up the stairs as the audience, once again, bounces their heads in unison.

Fast forward a few years later, a man comes up to me at intermission for a show and tells he me had been there before and saw "Dracula". My chest started to swell, but he smiled. "The night I saw it the bat flew into the audience."

My quick response (God, I could be good on my feet) was, 'Sorry, I didn't see it."

The story goes that Judy Garland, and her daughter Liza, attended a Broadway show. Judy apparently said a few things about the actress and her performance. Show's over and Judy stands up and tells her daughter they would go backstage and say hello. Liza asked her mother what she could possibly say? Judy swept into the room, beaming, and said, "How *do* you do it?"

For fun, I would use that line on friends from time to time and it became a running gag. When I went backstage to see a friend who knew the quote, the door opened and there were 5 women standing at their mirrors. "How *do* you do it?" I beamed. She looked at me, said, "Fuck you," and slammed the door. When I saw her later, we laughed so hard. She said the other women were silent for about five minutes, and then were told the joke.

Remember Grady? He called me to tell me he was going to be in his car as an extra in Guthrie for "Rain Man," starring Tom Cruise and Dustin Hoffman. I took my box office manager, LeAnn, closed the theatre, and drove to Guthrie. We stood on the sidewalk across from where they were filming the part when Dustin stops traffic. When the scene was over, Tom looked toward us. Actually, I think it was the preschoolers standing by us who came to watch. LeAnn and I shuffled closer to them. Tom picked up a little boy who leaned back, looking quizzically at Tom. We got Tom's autograph, and LeAnn asked if Dustin would come over. He said no, because he remained in character. The van pulls out with the actors. There sits Dustin. LeAnn suddenly pulled up her top to flash Dustin, as his head swung around in shock.

On a whim during our first trip to London, I decided to get my ear pierced. There was shop after shop. Linda and I stopped to see if we liked a certain shop and workers. From upstairs comes down this Arnold Schwarzenegger body, bald head, tattoos for days, in a white wife-beater (no pun intended). I grabbed Linda's arm, and we left. My Mama didn't raise no dummy. I knew he would pound that stud so hard into my ear that it would flatten like a pancake as if some tribe had initiated me into their fold.

At night, if I have to use the bathroom and get a drink of water, I always put a little water in the glass and empty it before re-filling. Just in case a spider, tarantula, or venomous, creepy/crawly thing snuck in.

Two things I demanded during my teaching career was to say "Please" and "Thank You," and be courteous to everyone. One day at Jarman Junior High, it had rained. Students entered, and as the bell rang, a student walked in. He was chubby, with red hair and freckles. His whole front was wet. I checked on him and started class.

After class, two cheerleaders told me that the three football players in class had pushed him down. You can only imagine how livid I was. No, you can't, so I will tell you. After school, I asked the counselor if he would, at the start of class the next day, call the student in for some made-up excuse. Over the intercom, the boy was asked to come to the counselor's office. Off I went! I must say, in my entire career of 29 years, I was foaming at the mouth as I told the class, glaring at the 3 bullies, that if it ever happened again, certain body parts of the offenders would be spread over 12 states. Never happened again.

Years later I got a call from him. He wanted to thank me for helping him and always being kind. He never knew of my tirade. I asked him what he was doing now. "I'm a professional wrestler and married with a little girl." Happy ending.

You want to see my wrath, be a bully. I would actually hear myself outside fuming my message, but inside I was telling myself to calm down. Did not work a few times. We should all be able to be ourselves with no help from anyone. Luckily, I did not have to deal with that issue a lot.

Two of my favorite books are "Boys and Girls Together," by William Goldman (why Netflix has not picked this up for a mini-series is beyond me), and "Naked Came I," on the life of sculpturer Auguste Rodin. A fascinating story in that for his first art show, he sculpted a life size statue of a nude soldier. At the show, very few people stopped to look at his work. He finally stopped someone and asked why they did not stop. He was asked how hard can it be to make a cast of a man?

From that day forward Rodin rarely used life-size again, but made exaggerated pieces to be bigger or smaller as a slam at his critics who had alleged he had cast the work of a living model. The work was titled "The Age of Bronze."

A few years later at the Metropolitan Museum of Art in New York City, there was a Rodin exhibit, and there stood the life-size soldier. I told my friend the story and heard light applause. I turned to see 12 people who had been listening, and asking if they could join my group.

Linda and I had only a handful of problems on our travels. In Italy I bought a small vessel with a lid. It was made of lead and stunning. As we went through security at the airport, I watched as my luggage went through the scanner. The woman looking at the screen froze, and her eyes went very wide. What now? She pulled another person over and he, too, had wide eyes. "Have you bought something that looks like a small vessel or something?" I said I had. They asked me if I would step back and look at the screen to confirm. Then *my* eyes went wide. It looked like a hand grenade! I took it out and showed them my lead treasure, much to their relief.

Embarrassing. When we arrived at the airport in Venice, we were told to take a taxi to our hotel. We stood there and waited, but to no avail. I suddenly laughed. Linda asked what was so funny? I told her they meant a water taxi, not a taxi with four wheels. Sheesh!! In our defense I will say there were automobiles behind us loading and unloading passengers for the airport or home or somewhere else. Four college age men saw our dilemma and offered to take us on their fishing boat to the hotel. They even took our luggage to our hotel. (Keep this story just between us).

In the 70's, my aunt and uncle in Kansas City had a party for their 50th wedding anniversary with approximately 125 guests. When introduced to people, rather than say I was a teacher, I thought it would sound more important if I said I was Production Director at the Jewel Box. Once I shook a hand and said Jewel Box, their hand slipped out of mine and their faces froze, and off they went. This went on for about 45 minutes until my uncle stopped the combo playing and explained to the crowd that I was Production Director of the Jewel Box Theatre in Oklahoma City. They turned to me and applauded. What the hell? My uncle came over and told me I got the reaction I did because the Jewel Box was a drag bar in Kansas City. After that, I was a teacher.

Sidebar: The Jewel Box Lounge in Kansas City still exists.

Boy, I sure can relate to women who have to shave their legs. When I was cast in the musical "Sugar," at Lyric Theatre, I played the part of Jerry/Daphne (the Jack Lemmon role in the movie "Some Like It Hot"). I had played the part twice at Jewel Box Theatre in Oklahoma City, not Kansas City, and wore dark hose instead of shaving. Director Lyle Dye, Jr. told me and the actor playing Joe that we would shave our legs.

Forty-two minutes! FORTY-TWO MINUTES to shave my legs with only two small cuts. Each leg was in every position possible in the sink during the torture. Men, ask your wives what a runner in your hose feels like. It happened to me on stage during a scene. The only good thing to come out of having to shave? A local television station critic said I had legs she was jealous of.

On Opening night there was always a party at a local venue. This one was to be held at a nightclub named Fuzzy's. I thought it would be fun to go as Daphne. I got a blonde wig at Jewel Box and a floor length fringe frock. To add to the merriment, I asked two twin brothers from school, who were bodybuilders, if they would go with me in costume. They agreed and wore the white and black sequined loin cloths my mother had made.

We met at the Jewel Box and off we went. It was a 15 minute drive. Two minutes into it, my mind froze. It's around 11:00pm at night. Drive the speed limit. Use turn signals. Stay in your lane. Your world is over if a cop pulls you over. I shiver thinking about my mug shot. Arrive. The boys take off their glasses, get out and drop to the pavement. I panicked. OMG, they dropped dead! Wait, they were just pumping up for their entrance.

In we go, standing at the top of the five stair entrance, me in the middle arm-in-arm with my escorts. Crowded. Music playing. No one looks. A few seconds and one of the boy's whispers, "What is going on?" I said we needed to quietly back up and run for our lives. Suddenly, those close to us spotted us and began to clap and cheer. Others joined in and the entire room was cheering. Friend Kerry Robertson came up and we had our picture taken exposing a leg.

Years later she found the picture and sent me a copy with the inscription: "Look at the gams on those two hams." We were a hit. Not sure, but in the history of Lyric parties, I don't think anyone has done something like that. The boys were happy. They got some girls' phone numbers.

Poor David. I directed the musical, "Mame," at Carl Albert High. In one of his lines David was to name an ingredient in a drink. My kids knew one thing you never do is laugh on stage. Ever. As David held up his glass, he said the secret ingredient was "Strained honey." That's what he was supposed to say.

What came out was "Strained horny." There was silence. The 3 actors on stage froze. I covered my mouth to hide my guffaw. One actor looked upstage at the start of the hint of a smile. Then another. I literally fell out of my chair in the auditorium, laughing, joined by everybody. Took a while to calm us down.

As fate would have it, he became a police officer, and as I walked out of the school office one day a few years later, he and another officer were coming up the steps. In a low tone he said, "Don't say a word." As we passed, I said, "No problem. I was just on my way to get some 'strained horny.'" We both burst out laughing.

My lucky number is 19. I don't know why because it has never impacted my life in any shape or form.

I swear, if my mother was alive, she would kill me over this one (again). But I can't help it. My aunt and uncle in Kansas City always said the bar at their home was open at 5:00 pm., where they sat with my parents and friends, and had drinks on their screened back porch. Although I never saw any of them drunk, they were a happy lot just before dinner. One time my aunt and uncle went to the country club where my aunt got sloshed. She was so drunk that when her steak came and she could not muster the utensils, she put her head on the table by the plate and started gnawing at the steak. (Sorry Mother, but I still think it's funny).

Not so funny was when mom, dad and my brother came up to have lunch with me on a Sunday when I was in college. I was under the weather as I had mirrored my aunt and gotten pretty drunk at a party the night before. When I smelled the food in the restaurant I felt my stomach start churning. I don't think my ghost-like white face helped any.

After the three ordered, the waiter looked at me. Dad smiled at me and said, "He'll have two Alka Seltzers." God love him.

Know what makes me feel good? Knowing I have so many students out there in all types of professions (Medical, Police, Lawyers, etc.) that I can call on for free help as needed.

Bathroom break.

* * * * * * * * * * * * * * * * * * * *

I'm back.

Power of suggestion. Now you go.

I get hooked when certain movies come on TCM: "To Sir With Love" is one. Why? Because I love it so much, and Sidney Poitier, I have to stop and watch, no matter where it is during the movie. However, after all these years I was watching To Sir, I asked myself: If Mr. Thackery is having so much trouble with the class, how on God's green Earth are the other teachers doing?? Especially Jillian, this sweet, tiny, meek woman. Think about it. Not once do the other teachers mention having the same trouble poor Mr. Thackery is having. What gives? Lost a little sleep over that one.

I love kids and the wonder they bring with them as they grow. At the high school we would produce a play every year and grade schools would be bussed in. 1,200 of them. We did "Snow White". When the witch came out the gasps from the kids and wiggling in their chairs made us happy. We had them engaged. At the end when the prince turned to walk away without kissing Snow White, a child yelled out, "You gotta' kiss her." Our Prince looked at the audience and said, "Thank you," and kissed her.

After the show I had the cast go outside the stage door and go to the lobby to meet the children as they exited. One side was stalled. What the...? A student on crew found me and told me the witch was outside that door, and kids did not want to be anywhere near her. She moved. As we were striking the set and all that, the janitor came up. "Must have been quite a show." He pointed to the front row on one side where I saw some puddles dotted along the row. "Some kids wet their pants."

Lawana Trout was to be my literature professor at college. She was coming off being named National Teacher of the Year while she taught in Sand Springs, and then transferred to Central State. Twenty-five of us sat there waiting for her entrance. She walked in, froze, looked at us and turned slowly, arms open wide and said, "I'm just an ordinary person." Who wouldn't love that?

She told us when she was going to the hotel where the ceremony was to take place in New York, she got on the elevator with a man she described as incredibly good looking. She kept peeking at him as they rode up. "Where are you going?" the stranger asked. When told the National Teacher of the Year banquet, he said he was, also. Into the big hall they walked and were suddenly swarmed. She was surprised because she knew three-fourths of the group did not know her. Apparently, they did know her elevator buddy. When asked if they knew each other, both gave a negative response. A woman said to Lawana she would like to introduce Leonard Bernstein.

She was one of only a handful of teachers who made my head hurt from absorbing everything she said. I have to share:

A. As an English teacher in New York, she graded papers, marking mistakes in red. And there were a lot of mistakes. She noticed that one day no one was writing. When asked, one explained why try when they were just going to see lots of red marks? She never used that color again, and I never used it when grading papers.

B. She had them keep diaries (which I did later for English classes). As they got ready for Open House, she was looking at the diaries. One girl proudly showed Mrs. Trout her diary, going into graphic detail how her prostitute mother had sex and drank and did drugs. The teacher put the notebook back on the desk and started to walk off. The student asked what she thought. Mrs. Trout said it was her diary, and if that was what she wanted, then all the parents could read it. She was in a panic at home and until she arrived early to school, to check on the diary. The graphic pages had been torn out.

C. In high school I had a low-level English class and copied Mrs. Trout. She let students write sometimes and there would be no grading. She gave us a photocopy of one story called, "The Case of the Missing Fingerprints." Mistakes galore, but what a fun, imaginative story, which never would have happened had she not allowed us the freedom to write. See why she was National

Teacher of the Year? We were so blessed to have had her.

Just saying: During my last 2 years of teaching in high school, I noticed some students could not spell on tests. I took some to an English teacher who told me that with computers there was auto correct. Blood is starting to boil. Let's boogie on.

Gerry Willingham was the librarian at First Christian Church where the Jewel Box was located. She told me that while in college she worked for a lawyer. She was at her desk outside his office when a man came up. His clothes were the worse for wear, he had not shaved in a couple of days, and some dead birds were hanging over his shoulder. She brought out the lawyer and took a break. When she came back, she asked who it was. Her boss apologized for not introducing her to Jim Thorpe! I quickly asked, "You did get an autograph, didn't you?" She did not.

Ever been sick and gone to work? Ever been sick and in a musical and have to go on, because in some community theatres there is no understudy? Of course, it was at the JB. I was playing Charlie Brown. Again, along with teaching school, being production director, and in a musical, I was worn out, and YIKES, my voice started going. I could rasp-talk, but not sing. Music Director Brian Tidwell suggested that he would sing, and I would mouth the words for two shows and then I'd have three days to rest up.

Got a reservation call. I told him he might want to wait a week as the actor playing Charlie Brown could not sing. He said he knew that, because he had talked to a friend who had seen it the night before and said it looked like a movie with Charlie Brown mouthing the words, and the piano player doing the singing. Audiences are the best.

At Carl Albert, the newspaper would come out first hour. Always a page where there were anonymous/silly things. One female wrote she wanted to take a certain young man to a desert island. I had him in first hour student council, but he was absent that day. The class laughed over what they thought his reaction would be.

During my second hour plan I was on the way to the office, and he was walking toward me. I stopped him and asked if he wanted to go to a desert island with me. Pause. Sure, he said. I was smiling, He had a lop-sided grin. We parted. A teacher came to me during second hour, and said they had had a good laugh in her class because the student was at the dentist first hour and did not see the paper. The next day students kept asking me if I wanted to go to a desert island.

You have to/have to/ have to Google Lydie Marland. It is one of the most interesting/bizarre/love stories I ever heard. Not enough time to tell it all, but she was born Lydie Miller Roberts. Her parents decided to give up Lydie and her brother for adoption as teenagers to their maternal aunt and uncle, Virginia and Ernest Whitworth Marland, who were both childless and very wealthy. So, the pair moved from Flourtown, Pennsylvania to Ponca City, Oklahoma.

Virginia Marland died in 1926, E.W., as he was called, annulled the adoption of Lydie Miller Roberts, and married her. She was 28 and he was 54. Lydie always called him E.W. He became Oklahoma's governor and after those who, shall we say, were a little on the matronly side (as reported), along came this vibrant, beautiful first lady. She was an instant hit.

Up to more present day. A friend dropped by my office and said she was coming from her book club where an author spoke of Lydie and said he had written a book and play about Lydie Marland. She gave me the script to read that he had given everyone. The author was Bob Perry.

I put it aside upon seeing it was very short and act one had 12 short scenes and act two about the same. Bored, one day I read it and almost exploded about the prospect of making this into a full-length play.

Took us almost a year, but Bob made this beautiful play about this complex woman into a thrilling play.

To try and see if anyone was still alive who might have known Lydie, I called David Keathley, executive director of the E.W. Marland estate. He gave me three names:

1. C.D Northcutt, an attorney responsible for getting Lydie back to Ponca City. Great story about that when you Google.

2. Betty and Charles Thompson, who lived on the property in a stunning house made from a stable that once housed Marland's prize horses.

Jana Hester, an invaluable friend, and I had the extraordinary pleasure of not only meeting all three, but having many chats that lasted for hours. They were so gracious.

You did not talk to Lydie first. When she would come over to Betty and Charles' house, she sometimes would have a can of cat food she needed Charles to open, when she could have opened it herself. She wore vintage clothes and got many a glance walking downtown, never talking to anyone. For her remaining days, she lived in the chauffeur's quarters where she had lived with E.W after they sold the property, and where he died. At 41 she was a widow. Lydie Marland died on July 5, 1987.

Could go on about Lydie, but it would be better to look her up or visit the museum.

We had the premiere of THE BROKEN STATUE on October 6, 2011.

The title comes from the fact that E.W. had statues made of both Lydie and her brother George. Lydie, upon deciding to leave Ponca City, paid a man to take the statue and destroy it. She wanted to watch him start, so he smashed the face which broke into pieces, but not completely shattered.

On his deathbed, the gentleman told his family that he had not destroyed the statue as ordered, but took it and buried it in a crate where no one knew where it was. In a drawer they found the location and went to dig it up two days before the company that owned the land was about to cement the lot.

The night "The Broken Statue" opened, the Thompson's, C.D. Northcutt, the mayor of Ponca City, and David Keathley were among the VIP guests. We had giant publicity, and the show sold out early on.

After a show, sometimes an audience member asked to talk to me with an E.W. story. One was a woman who said her uncle worked for E.W. When he lost Marland Oil, and it became CONOCO, E.W. gave expensive ties and suits to her uncle. Someone called the uncle, hearing he had the items, and said they would come get them as they were property of the company. When the men arrived to collect the valuables, they were taken to the backyard where the items were in a big barrel on fire.

* * * * * * * * * * * * * * * * * *

Scary story. It was a dark and stormy night. Oh, it was not. It was a warm summer night.

Being a new teacher, there was not a lot of money. I had an air-conditioner in the living room of my rent house and nothing in the bedroom. That will change, after all these years, once this book hits the bestseller list. Any-who, to try and stay cooler, I had the window open. I have to sleep with a sheet. So, my head was at the foot of the bed and my face was pretty close to the screen. I see a silhouette walking on my side of the street. It is around midnight. Dark dark.

Wearing an old fedora, head down, a man shuffles along. He stops. His body faces forward, but his head slowly turns to my window. (I have goose bumps right now remembering this. Really.) I pull my sheet up to just under my eyes. We all know if you are covered by your sheet, no harm can come to you. He shuffles toward my window. I stop breathing so as not to attract any attention to myself. At my window, he slowly bends over as he whispers, "Come here."

He is so close to the screen we are almost face-to-face. He picks up his little white poodle. "You come back here, you little rascal," and he shuffles back to the street, puts the dog down, and off they go. I thought I had wet the bed, but I had only sweated bullets.

One summer during college a friend got me a job with him at a nursing home. I would work the third wing where patients could not take care of themselves. I was on the night shift from midnight to 7 a.m. Some random happenings:

A. One night, early on, we heard this happy shouting of "Whoopee." The staff jumped up and started running down the hall. I followed. As Sherrie, the head nurse, started to open the door, she told me to step back. The others already had. When I could peek around, there stood the patient on his bed throwing feces all over the place. When you heard his joyous cry, it meant run. Welcome to work!

It was so easy to fall in love with the patients. When the manager came by once, she told me Sherrie told her how good I was with them. My simple reply was, "I treat them as I would want to be treated."

Try as you might, some patients wet/soil their underwear literally a few minutes after you would change and clean them up. A female staff had just checked on a woman who was dry. When a woman came in, everyone kind of stiffened. Sherrie said she could be a problem. Into her mother's room she went and was back out in like 15 seconds, demanding to know why her mother was wet. Sherrie took a step forward and I stopped her. Over I strode and, in no uncertain terms, politely explained someone was just in there and she was fine, so it had just happened, and we were taking care of her mother. Brief pause and she apologized.

One large non-verbal male was noted for, as you walked into his room to collect his urine sample, knocking over the plastic bottle with the urine splashing all over.

I told Sherrie one night I would gladly go in. Sure enough, as I walked into his room, he placed his hand against the bottle. I took one step. He pushed it slightly to the edge. I took two more steps and over it went. Well, he always had big books on medicine on his tray table to see why we were trying to 'kill him.' In one fell swoop, I pushed the thick books off of his table, and they crashed on the floor and hit the wall.

He tried to rise, hands out to strangle me. I stepped back, and he fell on the table and then the floor. Staff runs in. "What happened?" Innocent face as I say, "I don't know. He knocked the bottle over, I went to get it, and he fell." As they helped him up, he kept moaning loudly to try and get at me, arms flailing. He was not hurt in any way.

Next night. I am in the door. He sees me and up goes the hand to the bottle. I take one step. He pushes slightly. Another step and another push. I give him a grin. Lower my voice. "Go ahead. Knock it off. I dare you. (beat) I double dare you." Standoff. Slowly his hand goes to his lap. I take the bottle and say, "Thank you." If I went in to collect, all would be okay. Just part of the job, gang.

Dear sweet Ada Ray. She was a feisty woman, and I absolutely adored her and gladly went to her room if she was being disagreeable, because for some reason, I was the only one who could calm her down. It turned out that before I clocked out I had to go to Ada's room to get her out of bed. She would only do it for me, even while she groused, 'I don't want to. Stop it. Leave me alone', as I gently wrestled her out. Once she was in her wheelchair, she would look at me and take my hand and smile.

I had never seen anyone die. Sherrie asked me to help with a patient, whom she said would probably not last the night. She asked if I would be all right with it, and I said I would. I held her on her side while Sherrie rubbed lotion on her back to help soothe her dry skin. Eventually, we went in every 10 minutes, then Sherrie said it was almost over, so we stayed by her, while Sherrie held her hand.

As I looked at this old sweet face, she took her last breath. The funeral home was called, and at 5:30 in the morning, two young men came in giggling and having a good time. They took the gurney into the room, still having fun. As they wheeled her out of the room, Sherrie grabbed one and shoved him into the wall with these words: "You are handling a human being and she will be treated with respect. Do you understand me?" I looked down and thought (I might be wrong) that he was on his tiptoes. By now he was pure white and apologized. I hugged Sherrie, very impressed. My reward was she pushed me jokingly away and barked, "Back to work."

One quiet night, I got bored and me and the other five people on the wing decided I would put on a patient's robe (like at the hospital, open in the back), and go out the door in the second wing, and have the staff come out and try and bring me in. Bad move, in that it started to drizzle as I walked out, the red light on to indicate the door was open. I shuffled around as I mumbled. The second wing nurse was at the door pleading for me to come back in. I shuffled in the drizzle. I slowly walked back, head down. She still did not know it was me. As I came in, I turned to the first door on the right and started to enter. We pretty much knew those patients, too. The nurse grabbed my arm and told me I could not go in there, that it was Mrs. Smith's room (shall we say). I cackled, "I know," and with a frozen face, she jerked me around. The hidden staff popped up laughing. What I got for my charade was a swat on the butt.

I treasured my time there and actually visited Ada Ray in the hospital when she had an operation. Still feisty!

I think it's funny when ordering, people ask, 'May I have the (fill in the blanks)? I would love to be a waitperson so I could say, "Hell, no, you may not. Get out of here! You have some nerve."

I use Google a lot but don't understand how one can ask for something and it pops up in seconds. Where did they get it? When asking for a clip from something, most of the time it pops up. Is that not copyrighted? It's in the cloud I am told, to which I reply what the hell is a cloud holding all this information and which cloud is it in? Mysteries abound.

For my Central State University graduation, I did not want to go and have to listen to lots of Rah Rah speeches, AND to have to wait until they got to the T's would be more than I could bare. Mom and Dad had scheduled a trip to Kansas City to visit my aunt and uncle after graduation so they could watch Buddy Boy walk across the stage. He did it! I told them I had no plans to attend, so they bought three plane tickets, and then I found out it was required to be there (I think).

I met with a counselor and told him I could not attend as I had a job interview in Kansas City and showed him the ticket. I flew out one happy camper. Did not miss it and I never got a high school class ring, either. We lived comfortably, but our parents did not have large amounts of cash lying around. I told them, when they offered to buy me a class ring, that I did not want one. I knew from where I had graduated, and did not need to look at a ring to verify it. Just me. Never regretted it.

Speaking of my school challenges, when I made the Dean's Honor Roll at CSU, they sent my parents a letter of congratulations. In college, learning became more fun (minus science and a few of those classes). I walked in the house and Dad had the letter in his hand and showed it to me. I smiled. He did not, but asked me who I was cheating off of. Oh, that country boy humor. Gets me right here (as I pat my butt).

My first movie role! I worked at Lynn Hickey Dodge for one summer, and he came to me one day and said I had mentioned theatre, and he had something for me. He took me to the front door. They were filming a movie called, "The Only Way Home." As the two stars drove out of the parking lot, Lynn and I stood at the door and looked at them quizzically.

Went to see it and the last name in the credits was mine. Chuck Sweet.

Maye ran the switchboard at that dealership, and I got to help her, as I did down the street at another car dealership. This one, however, was so old fashioned that it had plugs. When I would (on some occasions) accidentally unplug them, when they called me to ask what happened, I told them they were still plugged in, and they disconnected apparently. We called back or they did.

For April Fool's Day, I had Maye call my mother at home and ask if she would accept a "collect call." I got on the line and told her I was in jail in Kansas and needed money. Big sigh and mom asked how much? I told her the joke. Suddenly the phone went dead. I had a party a few weeks after that, and as fate would have it, Mom and Maye were back-to-back, but chatting with other people. My mother turned and tapped Maye on the shoulder and said her voice sounded familiar. Maye explained her job. Mother smiled. "I'm Chuck's mother, and I recognized your voice asking me if I would accept a collect call." Had a good laugh over that one, and they actually kept in touch for a few years.

In the early days of teaching, we were free to galivant all over. For example, my kids filmed a soap opera called Grey House, and it appeared on the new Cox network where the office was close to school. We would film and two students would go to Cox and edit, and it would appear on television. What a thrill.

Some Soap Opera facts:

In one episode, a student jumps off the roof of his house and lands in the pool knocked "unconscious." We drove to the ER and were going to sneak around and film there. Maybe disappear into a room and show him in bed where he was supposed to die. Suddenly, a Doogie House doctor (maybe 15 years old tops) came up and asked what we were doing. I explained, and he said he wanted to help. He guided us to an area with all the hook ups. He called in a nurse, and she stood by to 'help.' He was an actual doctor. He told the camera person that when he slightly nodded his head, the camera should pan up to the monitor that was showing a heartbeat. Slight nod. Camera pans up and the heart rate flatlines. He had taken off the apparatus on the actor's chest to show the flatline. Great cliffhanger.

Same for a big grocery store just down the street from the school. Talked to the manager who said we could film a scene where two students rob the place. She had only one stipulation: she wanted to be behind the counter to be robbed. Per these cases, I had two students at the front door to alert patrons we were filming a movie. Everyone was so into it that the door guards did not notice a little old lady shuffling in with her cane. The blank gun went off, and we heard a scream as the old lady about fainted. We rushed to her. She was fine. Note to self: Slap door guards.

One of my very favorites was with the help of colleague, Brenda Bodenheimer. She taught with me, and her husband Eddie was a Colonel in the Air Force and a pilot. So, he approved flying in his Cessna with a student, himself, and the cameraman in the tiny back seat. The cliffhanger was for the student to hear his motor sputter and call out 'Mayday." When I saw the clip, it was truly breathtaking. The plane motor spits. My student has one hand on the controls, and the camera is on him and not Eddie, so it looks like the student is flying. In the other hand is a microphone. After the 'Mayday" call, the plane banks to the right and...blackout. We got so many calls and letters telling us how much they enjoyed our soap opera.

Sidebar: When filming at a student's house we needed an extra. Kristin called her boyfriend to come over. He did not want to do the bit, but he did it for her. So glad Mike Gundy (head football coach at Oklahoma State University) was there that day and thanks to his girlfriend and now-wife, Kristin. She was one delightful student who smiled constantly.

When I come back, I would love to be a dog for either my brother Lindsey, or Bestie, Jan Garrett. Talk about a dog's life! I love how they talk to them as if the dog would reply with an intelligent answer. Too funny. I know they are their children.

I was always looking for fun, informative things for my students. When I read a story about a teacher who took her class to a nursing home and let the students talk to residents, I knew I had to do it, too. When I announced my brilliant idea, I was met with scowls, growls and beady eyes. Having 51 percent of the vote, off we went to a nursing home close to the school. For the entire 45 minutes, I walked the halls observing it all. I stopped when I saw, with their backs to me, a big football player sitting by a little old lady who had her left arm on his back. When it was time to depart, I went to that room. The student, in tears, was outside the room with his head on the wall. I gave him a pat on the back. He said, when he sat down, she asked if it would be all right if she watched the last of her soap opera, which was 10 minutes.

The next day I asked who wanted to go first with the story of their patient. Every hand flew up, yelling for me to choose them. They were in awe with stories of the dust bowl, turning a crank to start a car, and no heat, air-conditioning, and no phones.

A month later a student asked me if I knew what the football player had been doing. After my negative reply, he said the player was visiting his new friend every two weeks on Sunday.

The best laid plans and all that jazz. What a life-changing challenge I thought up. I was directing the thriller, "Wait Until Dark" at the JB, and thought how much we take our sight for granted. I decided to blindfold students and take them outside, and they had to find their way back. I chose four students to help wrangle them, blindfold them and down the back steps we went. They were everywhere as Mr. Tweed kept checking on their welfare. Instructed them as best I could, "Keep your hands moving back and forth as you walk." Some still walked like Frankenstein and smacked (gently) into a pole or standing object. Most were pretty much at the back stairs, and I heard a muffled, "Hello." Not yelling, just talking. I scanned the practice football field. Nothing. There it was again. As I walked toward the softball dugout where workers had, earlier in the day, started digging post holes for the new lights. There, with his blindfold still on, stood a student in the hole. "Anyone there?" He had fallen into a six foot deep hole.

I pulled him out, but he refused to take his blindfold off, as he said it would not be the same experience.

"I'm so hungry I could eat a horse." "I'm so hungry my stomach thinks my throat has been cut." This experiment was to come to school for a day and not eat all day or night but have breakfast the next morning.

Cheaters were reported to me, and I found a couple of students sneaking food off plates in the cafeteria. I went home to find my wife had made this beautiful steak. (Forgot to tell her about fasting). My stomach was in knots. We all survived but, "I'm so hungry," took on a whole new meaning.

Big movie buff. Especially scary ones, and I love scaring people, which probably goes back to being a pushed over triangle.

Take the movie "Halloween." One of my favorites. The audience is so busy screaming they don't actually think through what just happened. For example, when Laurie opens a bedroom door to discover Lynda's dead body on the bed with a big, marble headstone on the headboard. Come on. How in holy horror did killer Michael Myers get that bugger out of the graveyard, up the stairs, and on the headboard all by himself?

You don't have time to think, because when Laurie sees that in horror, she backs up to a closet where Lynda's boyfriend, Bob (killed earlier) swings out of the closet toward Laurie and the audience. Big scream. But...BUT how did Michael prop Bob up in the closet so he would swing out upside down? The clothes bar would not hold his weight. What was holding poor Bob up? Rigor mortis must have set in pretty fast. AND, when he came out swinging (so to speak), bad Bob doesn't even fall to the ground. Not laughing because we were too busy screaming. Knowing that valuable information I just gave you, in no way hinders me from enjoying that movie.

* * * * * * * * * * * * * * *

I like to laugh at people who stand at a busy intersection and keep poking at the cross button as if the light won't ever change.

* * * * * * * * * * * * * * * * * *

When my grandfather farted in an elevator full of people and it started to smell, he would turn to my grandmother, touch her shoulder and ask, "Are you alright?"

They had a pet skunk named Petunia, and my grandfather didn't inform new visitors, so he could see their reaction. Of course, everyone about bolted through their big picture window in fear.

 Granny told me Grandpa said they needed a new car, and she should go to the dealership where they bought all of their cars and pick one out. She did and turned to leave. The salesman handed her the keys, and she was confused. She was told grandpa had left a blank check so she could get the car she wanted.

Granny once asked me why I would sit for hours listening to his stories. How could I not, as "J.J. Johnny Madden" told me about his being a professional golfer and in the oil business? He was the golf professional at both the Oklahoma City Golf and Country Club and Hidden Valley Family Golf course. He pulled out pictures of him posing with some golfers who looked vaguely familiar, but so young. He would point to a picture with such famous names as Ben Hogan, Sam Snead, and Arnold Palmer, among others.

A friend of his broke his arm turning the crank on a Model T, which backfired, jerking his arm out of place.

My grandfather, brother, and brother-in-law were excellent golfers and won a few tournaments. Not me. Try as I might that white ball would not go where I was looking. For example, one time I smacked the ball off the tee and down the fairway. Only I did not see it flying down the fairway as planned. My grandfather pointed to my right. What I had hit landed on the ninth hole as opposed to going to the first hole where I was aiming. Guess who never picked up another club?

Like Halloween, it's also fun to watch ads and wonder if. (After I finish this spellbinder, I need to get a life). Try this one (with no brand names mentioned).

A young couple is standing in the snow in the middle of nowhere. He says he has a gift for her and turns and whistles. Out of the snow bounds this adorable puppy, happily approaching, bouncing in the snow. She says she has a surprise, too. She whistles and barreling out of the snow comes a truck. The snow flies beautifully around the new vehicle. Which begs the questions: Where did the dog come from? Was he sitting in the snow waiting? Did someone hold him until they heard a whistle and shoved him out? More importantly, who in the hell is driving the truck??? And, what happens to the driver once the man throws himself on the hood and hugs it? Makes one wonder, doesn't it? Or not.

I will admit it. It makes me laugh when a mishap happens to someone. Not a horrific accident or anything. I don't want to see anyone hurt. For example, my wife and I were shopping. She was pushing the cart. As we turned the corner, SPLAT!. A woman tripped and fell on top of her child/grandson, and we saw this woman face down on top of a little boy, his arms and legs sticking out on the sides, flopping up and down. Neither were hurt. We lost it. I was crying go hard I had to bend over. I walked away from our cart, and a few steps down the aisle, some people came to see what was going on. Still in hysterics, I turned and leaned into our cart laughing. I looked up, and there stood a woman I did not know who was not laughing. It was not our cart. Behind her, my wife was laughing hysterically.

Went to see the musical "The Fantasticks." The show is very intimate, but because of the big stage they had put some scaffolding to fill the space. As an actor began to sing "Soon It's Gonna' Rain", the mime, up on the scaffolding, began to sprinkle confetti that floated down and some went right into the actor's open mouth, titled upward as he sang. He bent over and began to gag as he tried to continue singing. I lost it.

Intermission. Went to restroom. Standing there, doing my business, an old man came in and stood next to me. Suddenly, I snorted and laughed out loud. "Soon it's gonna..." He quickly finished, washed his hands and left. When I opened the door to come out, he was standing with his wife and pointed at me and said, 'That's' him.' Went back to my seat. Woman behind me whacked me on the shoulder and hissed, "I hope you control yourself for the rest of the show." I did. But, only because there were no more mishaps. I swear, some people.

I try to be a good traveler. One thing I do hate is when the plane gets up in the air, and the seat in front of me immediately comes back. No matter that sometimes they sit up and do not even lean back. When we got served food, I would reach between the seats and tap the person and tell them to put up their seat back so I could eat!

I may or may not have caused permanent damage when a foot (bare/stinky/toe fungus, etc.) would appear on an arm of my seat. I would simply lean my elbow on the offender, who yelped and moved it.

Talk about heaven! We were boarding our return plane from Bora Bora. I turned to the right to go to our economy seats. I bumped into the steward, who looked at my ticket and said we were upstairs. Eureka! In business class for eight luxurious hours. Waited on hand and foot.

Whoever waits on a foot? You lucky dogs who get to travel like that all the time.

With all that is going on now, my travel days are over, but oh what a fun time I had. Might share some more in volume two of snippets. Not really. I'm a one book wonder.

Imagine my surprise when I found out the final section of the college yearbook was to be driven to Kansas City, where the staff would have dinner at the Playboy Club. Stepping into the elevator and looking down at the Playboy logo on the carpet got my heart racing. The elevator doors open, and there you are, just taking it all in. After years of reading the magazine and what comes with it, to see this place was surreal. We sat down. Up came the Bunny, who backed into the table with her hip, to take our order. That way, the Bunny did not have to bend over and therefore avoided a double disaster falling out.

At the next table, (big surprise) was a drunk, loud, obnoxious man. Each time the Bunny came over, he was inappropriate. She handled it like a pro, sweetly telling him he was not to touch the Bunnies. He would just cackle as if she was flirting. He reached across her back, put his hand on her hip, and pulled her in. Every so slightly, she looked at the entrance where several men (who apparently left their coat hangers in their coats with those big shoulders), stood. She tilted her head ever so slightly for him to come over, and over one came, tapped the man on the shoulder, and I do mean tap, and politely, in a calm voice, asked him not to touch the Bunny. Gulping, sweating, and stammering, he agreed and apologized. I will never forget that slight tilt of her head to bring over the bouncer. Truly an experience.

Only once in my lifetime have I been called to jury duty. I was actually pretty excited to be able to sit on a jury and do my civic duty. As people got dismissed for this or that, I remained. A lawyer asked a person, "Which is worse? Sending an innocent man to prison, or letting a guilty man go free?" The prospective juror answered. The next person asked, chose the opposite side. Then he came to me, and I said, "Neither. I think both are reprehensible." The second person that had answered raised her hand. She was acknowledged. "I changed my mind and agree with the last gentleman." There went jury duty. Rats.

Obviously, during basic training you get to know each other well. We all agreed this one person had the most beautiful teeth. (Bored, were we?) Since I knew him pretty well, they wanted me to go in and see what he was using for those perfect molars. No! More prodding and off I went, going to pretend I was brushing my teeth. I kept trying to sneak a peek and then got uncomfortable and stopped sneaking. He put down his brush. Smiled. "Is there something you want to ask me,

Tweed?" Stammer. I said we wanted to know what he used. Cupped in his hand was a bar of Ivory Soap with a dent down the middle where he rubbed his toothbrush. He offered some. I declined. Went back and reported, and six soldiers gulped. Okay, later I tried it, gagged, and threw away the bar.

With a new camera, off Linda and I went to Nice, France. We always loved going out for a few hours to tan. We would be out around 10 a.m. Five lounge chairs away on the beach was this older woman on her back. So what? Well, she had no top on, which one can do there, each sagging breast rested comfortably on each side. I got on the other side of Linda and pretended I was taking a picture of her, but in reality, I was aimed for the laid-out woman. It was not malicious, but that this woman was so free. Why not use the panoramic shot since I had never tried it? I wanted a memory of her being able to enjoy life.

I went to pick up my pictures at the drugstore. The woman brought them to the counter, stifling a smile. Another woman from the camera department came up. "We enjoyed your beautiful pictures. Especially this one." Out came, in a glorious panoramic view, my pinup on the lounger.

You just can't make this up!! As stated, both my mother and sister died of COPD. Dad had called us to tell us to come over, it did not look good for Mom. Family and friends were in the den. My sister, who had been there all night, said she and her husband would go home, shower and return. My brother left shortly thereafter. Standing in the room with me was my aunt, who said, "You know when she will go, Buddy? When someone is in the room who can take it." Never heard that. She left and I sat by the bed. I touched Mom's chest to be sure there was a heartbeat, but I could not tell because she was very thin. I got Dad and, after checking, he said she was fine. In the time it took Dad to go back to the den, Mother passed with just me in the room.

Oh, it ain't over yet. Get the Kleenex ready. Not to cry, but to laugh. My sister was livid that she did not stay and sped back up to the house. A hospice nurse had arrived and was sitting by the headboard, asking questions and making notes. My sister was wiping tears. I finally asked if she was okay. Blubbering, she said the last thing mother wanted was for her to blow cigarette smoke into her face. Imagine the room temperature dropping from a comfortable 68 degrees to about minus ten below.

The worker turned to stone as I slowly turned to my sister, thinking she must be speaking in tongues. What the...? I could just see it. "Here, Mother, this is for you." POOOH. And I laughed. Boy, did I laugh. Boy, did my sister get mad. So mad she left the room. The worker began writing again. "How many times you hear that one?" We both cracked up.

Sis and I were running down the street with some grade school friends as some birds flew over, and she said the poem, "Birdie, Birdie, you are grand, please don't do it on my hand." It did. Glad she didn't say, "Birdie, Birdie, in the sky, please don't do it in my eye."

When asked if I could have one power, what would it be, my immediate reply was, "Who gives a flying flip? Ain't gonna' happen, so don't ask me."

Being invisible.

One day I walked into the speech office in college to see a friend, saw a script, and picked it up. It was a children's play that was going to tour some of the grade schools. I read a few lines of Kevin, the leprechaun who is the narrator, in my best Irish accent and left. My friend immediately called me at the dorm and asked me to come back. I had read, and the graduate student directing the play heard me and asked me if I would like to be Kevin.

I had the prettiest Irish green corduroy suit with pants at the knee and white tights. Had never toured before so was a little anxious to see what the reaction would be. No need to have worried. They loved it and being able to talk to the actors, as instructed, was joyful to watch. One performance, I noticed a little girl to my right. She kept looking at my knee as I sat cross-legged. I caught her after the fifth time and indicated to watch the show. She looked at her friend and put her finger up. The friend nodded yes. Her finger ever so slowly reached over and touched my knee. She quickly showed her friend, and they touched fingers and giggled while I smiled.

After the show we talked to the kids. I was Kevin, a cobbler, and some kids showed me their shoes and asked if I made them. Of course, I did. Another time I was bent over at a desk, signing my name on a program and got pinched on the butt. Kevin turned to the giggling offender and said that was a No-No.

New Orleans. Ah, I love visiting that city. What could possibly happen there of note?

How about this? My brother lived just outside New Orleans and invited me down for Mardi Gras. We were packed on Bourbon Street like 'sardines in a tin.' We kept getting separated by people walking between us, with us, around us, and offering us a wide assortment of...(fill in the blank). So packed we did not/could not walk side by side. I took my brother's hand and said to hang on.

His hand slipped out of mine and without turning, I reached back and grabbed it again. One block later I turned to find out I had been holding some drunk college guy's hand. I immediately let go. He, swaying, asked me, "Where we going?" Behind him stood my brother laughing. I told him I was going on down the street, and we left the poor soul.

Went to a theatre conference there and got to meet author Robert Harling, who wrote "Steel Magnolias," and who was a wonderful guest speaker. The movie was being made at the time. We were going to produce it at the Jewel Box and my wife was going to play Truvy. In some of our programs, I got celebrity autographs of actors who had starred in the show or movie, as well as celebrities. His would be perfect. I had a prepared piece of paper that said congratulations and his signature. It's much more special if they add a note. He stood there and leaned into my wife's ear, then wrote something while they both laughed. She relayed he wrote, "May your hairdo's be perfect." Only he asked her how to spell hairdo.

I did not realize I was a picky eater until it was brought to my attention.

Turns out I am, but do not apologize for it. Rather than give you a list, let me tell you this. I hate hate hate liver and onions!!!!! Clever me. When mother made it, I would chew some, put my napkin to my mouth, put the offensive taste and smell into the napkin, and put it under the table for the dog. He was one healthy dog. Years later, when talking about food, my mother interjected that I was not as clever as I thought, by telling me she knew the dog was being fed under the table. Foiled again.

Mother usually made dessert for dinner. I'm not a fan of lemon meringue. I like meringue, but not lemon. In junior high, one night at dinner, just as my sister was lifting the meringue to her mouth, country boy dad threw in, "You know, meringue looks like calf slobber." Down went sis's fork, and for the rest of her life, she would shove the dreaded meringue to the side and eat the lemon part. I took the meringue and gave her the lemon.

Mother was not amused when dad told the story of when they first got married and she made noodles, which he promptly shot back at her, like rubber bands. They were that snappy.

How spooky is this? When I turned on my computer to get back to the grind, there was a poll on "Are you a picky eater?" Big Brother at work.

Must be inherited from mother. I don't drink water unless it has something in it like you can buy to make it not taste like water.

About time for the tug-at-your-heart moment in the narrative. The story of the pain and suffering I endured for eight weeks to get back my health. I am so full of shit. Didn't happen that way. But I digress.

One Friday I was at the Jewel Box taking reservations. I was supposed to be by myself, but my good friend Joan Corbin came in to work on the next program. She came on Tuesday and Wednesday to help after her day job.

I was talking to a customer and, with pencil in hand, writing down information. Suddenly, the pencil began to make strange marks on the page, and I realized I was slurring my words. Then I could not write at all. I hung up and asked Joan to drive me to the emergency room. By the time we got to her car, I felt relatively normal. What had just happened?

She dropped me off at the emergency entrance and went to park. One lady was at the counter, three more were working on computers, their backs to us. I simply said, "I'm having chest pains," and suddenly there were seven people around me hooking me up, talking to me. The ER doc said it looked like I had had a mini stroke, and was back, more or less, to normal.

Admitted. Shuffling along. When meeting the doctor for the operation, I had one request: to make the scar as invisible as possible so I could still wear my Speedo to the pool. He sat frozen, then laughed. And I'll be darned if you can barely tell there is a scar, and NO, I don't wear a Speedo at my age.

The staff was incredible at the hospital. When I awoke, I was ready to beg for lots of drugs to ease the pain. Except, there was no pain. None. Went home and prepared to have excruciating pain for weeks, months and years. Never happened. Bypass times five. Not because there was blockage in all the veins, but doing the five would give me 12 or so more years. Still here. Only the good die young. The new six million dollar man with a barely visible scar.

In the 5th grade I had had enough of my parents and told them I was leaving. Mother took me to my room and packed a small suitcase. Mom and Dad walked me to the door and wished me good luck. Hold that thought. This is the part where they were supposed to beg me to stay, and they would have no rules for me. I'll show them. I started down the steps as I heard the front door close. It was around 6 p.m., getting dark. Up the street I go (10 houses away) and get to the corner. Now what? I look down the street, shocked my parents weren't running up the street, arms outstretched to grab me, smother me with kisses and go home. Steet lamp comes on. No parents. No ride. No prospects.

Slowly I walked home. I bet they got the message. They were not on the porch. I went into the den where they sat watching television. I informed them it was too late to leave, and I would go another time. They said, "Okay," and mother told me to put my clothes back in my dresser. You know the end of that saga: Never tried that again.

Turns out in later years, everyone wanted to come to my house because my parents were "cool." Yuk.

If you would indulge me for a moment, I would like to tell you about my dad, Bill Tweed. Adoptive, but I never met or knew good ole' Charlie. Dad was one of the kindest people I ever met, and I treasured my times with him. He never got mad, BUT when he looked at you and spoke softly to warn you about something, it was like a stake in the heart.

So gentle that, when in grade school he would call us in for a spanking (Sis went first). He would "spank" us, we would give Academy Award-winning performances with our crying, walk out of the room, stop the act, and go back to what we were doing. Imagine my surprise when, one day, my sister came out and was actually crying. I asked what was up, but she could not stop whimpering. Dad called me in, and I proceeded to get over his knee, but he stopped me and had me sit beside him. Huh? He explained that since I was in the fifth grade, he was disappointed in me in that, at this age, I still needed a spanking. (Cue the waterworks). He said he hoped this would be the last time we had this discussion, and I went to my sister's room where we laid on her bed and cried together. Smooth-talking country boy knew his stuff.

My sister was a reporter for the Bomber Beam, the school newspaper, and was very good at it. Sometimes the local paper had student's articles on the school page, and there she was. Very proud of her.

Brother, as stated, was an exceptional football/baseball player. Proud of him, also. Dad not only attended, but later was on the sidelines, holding the pole that indicated what down it was. I don't do this sport so have no idea what it's called. Could Google, but on a rampage to get to the next snippet.

And then, good ole' dad attended plays, with his son chewing the scenery.

At JB, I made sure dad was in an aisle seat for my play. I made an agreement with the director, that when I was supposed to sit on an audience member's lap, I would go up three rows and sit on Dad's. Big laughs. Even more when he shoved me off and I landed on my ass.

I was Master of Ceremonies with partner Saundra Dowden at CSU for the annual Bronze and Blue Review (talent show). To introduce each act, we performed a short skit. For one bit, I told the family, who took up the entire 15 seats on the row, that when I ran up, everyone was to shift to the left so I could run through. Got there. Dad smiled and did not move. Mother gently swatted his legs but too late. Saundra, chasing me, was almost there. I stepped on dad's knees and down the aisle I went. We need to have a chat on how to not upstage his talented son.

This is how much my father was beloved. Some friends and I were out driving around. Not drinking, etc., just driving around. I looked at the time. It was almost midnight and that was my curfew. I told the driver to pull over and explained why. The entire car started talking baby talk: "Does Buddy have to call his daddy? Can't Buddy stay out a little longer?" I told them to drive on as I started planning my funeral.

Got home around 12:20 a.m. Best friend was with me as I opened the back door. Dad was sitting in his chair reading a Zane Grey novel. He looked up and said, 'You're grounded," and went back to reading. Joey said good-bye and left. Grounded? What was that? It was, actually, not being able to go out, no television, and no extra anything. I had never been grounded.

On Tuesday Joey called me. (Like jail, I was allowed one phone call). I asked why he was not out with the guys? He said he was grounded. "How? Your parents were okay with the small delay."

"Remember," he said, "when your dad said we were grounded?" Are you kidding me? Shows how much respect he had for dad. Dumb, but had respect for Dad.

There are many examples I could give about him, but you get the picture. He lived six years longer than Mom and never married again, or saw anyone. He said he was waiting to join my mother.

Oh, to be more like Bill Tweed.

Right on cue, one night many years ago my phone rang, and I was asked if I was Charles Tweed.

"This is…This is Charles Warfield," the voice on the phone said. And the hits just keep o-n-n-n-n coming. He got my number from mom, who was a sneak, and never told us they communicated whenever Charlie felt like it. Far and few between. Mother never said one bad word about Charlie.

So, for two hours we chatted. He said he knew that Bill was considered my father, and he accepted it. I interrupted and said, no need to discuss it further because Bill was my father.

He invited me out to California. He was married with a son named (Drum roll), Charles. At the time, being a poor teacher, I declined. I do regret not making time to go. Would have been interesting to talk to the great con man. Like "Catch Me if You Can," with all the role playing. Granny said he could have been a millionaire (drat the luck) if he could have just focused. She also said Charlie called mother the love of his life. Quite the quote for a man who had so many kids and wives.

Speaking of kids. Sis told me (when we were older) that Mother told her Charlie had called the high school to see if he could check her out for lunch. Office said no, because he was not on the checkout list. What was I? Chopped liver?

We had 4 phone calls over the month, each about two hours. Then stopped.

RIP Charlie.

The reason I loved teaching drama so much was because I knew most of them would not go into drama, but they would appreciate it in many mediums.

Yet, four have surprised me and chose that field in speech, theatre, and movies. One happy camper to have them share the same passion I had been given by Mrs. Garten.

Let's talk baseball, about which I knew very little. When I got to Jarman Junior High to teach drama, the program was almost non-existent. Same for when I first started at Carl Albert High, and ending my career at Del City High.

The principal at the junior high informed me I would be coach/assistant coach for either football, basketball, or baseball. I told him I knew nothing about any of them. He said to choose one. I said 8th grade baseball because my dad had coached my brother's team and knew he would help.

Gladly, my brother joined in when he could. I watched and tried to learn at a break-neck speed. Dad had those boys really shaping up. We immediately started winning games. Then I was called into the principal's office and told a father wanted me replaced as I was not a real coach. Three other fathers shared the same concern. I agreed, but told him about dad, and he knew they were a winning team. Skip to the end, in which we emerged as conference champs or some such honor. (Thanks dad and bro).

One day during class there was a knock on my door. When I opened it, there stood the student whose father wanted me gone. He stammered that there was a sports banquet at the end of the year, and I was invited. I said no, adding, I was glad I would never have to talk to them again and closed the door. (Real mature, but I did not care). I must say, not all the players and dads were against me. Around six should cover it.

I tried to be a good person. Help everyone. Be a good teacher. Play well with others. You cannot even imagine my shock when I came back the following year to find eight of the players had enrolled in drama.

They came in, all happy, saying hello. My first words for them: You are now in my playpen, and I know what I am doing. One player said they knew that, and they really liked my dad, brother, and me. Needless to say, they were really good at drama. My good luck.

The pitcher could throw so fast that if you blinked you missed it. Only one thing: Dad felt he was throwing wrong and would ruin his arm. He worked privately with him and although, at first slow, he got better. Dad told me he saw him a few years later and the pitcher said when he moved up, they told him to throw the old way because it was faster. Thus, ended his dreams for professional baseball. He ruined his arm.

The principal came to me at the end of the year and told me what an excellent job I had done. I really appreciated that. I had built up the drama program so that was all I taught. He became one of my biggest supporters. Some laughs on that coming up.

Pet Peeve: Not being kind

Star Sign: Leo. Surprised?

Chocolate or vanilla? The latter

Favorite food: Picky eater picks steak, medium-well, thank you

Something always on my shelf: At least 3 flavors of Bigelow tea

Biggest fear: Not much if I see it first

Favorite saying: (Darn, I hope I get to say it one day), is by Edward Gibbon: "I never make the mistake of arguing with people for whose opinion I have no respect." Oooo, mic drop.

Least favorite food: See previous liver story. Ick. Sputter. Burp.

Most embarrassing moment: Like I'd tell that one, but it does involve 6 kegs of beer, weed, Crisco, 150 people and...Oh, hell, did not happen

I am the proud recipient of an Oklahoma 2013 Governor's Arts Award for my contribution to the arts presented by the Oklahoma Arts Council and given to me by the Governor. It was a highlight of my life. Hang around long enough and...

When I started teaching, my mother asked me how I could teach with my temper. I asked her to come watch. I told the class she was a visitor from the Administration Building. It was a speech class so lots of chatter, etc. After class, mother said she did not know how I did it. I told her they were super. She said she would pinch their heads off and tell God they died. (Don't you love the old sayings?)

Little did I realize when I started teaching, the extent to which I would be in their lives, and they in mine. They become our children, too, wanting nothing but the very best for each and every one.

Don't ask me how or why, but for some reason, if there was a 'troubled' male student, he ended up in a class of mine, put there by the counselors because they felt I might be able to help. Like the time I was called to the office where the junior high vice-principal was talking to a student I had, but who was disruptive in some other class.

Suddenly, this thin short student bolted out of the office and a side door, with me in hot pursuit. As I grabbed for him, he wrapped himself around a pole on the breezeway, and I wrapped myself around him. After a few attempts to get free, he turned his head to me and spat out: "Fuck you."

I replied, 'You wouldn't like it, I just lay there."

He stopped, looked at me, smiled, and said, "Let's go back in." The rule became, as with a few others, that if the student started having a meltdown, he was allowed to leave the room and come sit in my class. When the vice-principal called the mother and said they were sending the child home, she begged for him to be kept at school, because if he was sent home he would be beaten by the father. He stayed.

During high school, a teacher came to my room and said I was wanted in the VP's office. When I entered, he told me the male student had wanted me there. There were three chairs opposite the VP's desk. In the far left chair, the mother, with a hanky, crying. Center chair, her son. I stood there while the VP explained the mother was having trouble with her son and was asking for help. A sob from her.

The son said, "She's such a bitch." He suddenly shot forward as I slapped him on the back of his head. He felt his head and said, 'You hit me."

"'And I will again if you ever talk to your mother like that again."

The VP, meanwhile, was babbling something like, "Uh, Mr. Tweed, we don't hit the students." I told him this one didn't count. He began to melt in his chair like the Wicked Witch of the West in "The Wizard of Oz".

The solution? Mother or son could call me day or night. Calls from her were regarding having to sleep on the couch by the front door so he could not sneak out, but he would use his bedroom window. His complaint was her constantly nagging him about something. (Some big, some small). That went on for two months until they finally made it work and respected each other. No charge.

Back then there was a class called Special Education. A good friend taught a class. Second semester, one of her students sat there in my stagecraft class. I do admit he had quite the reputation for being explosive, but a darn good football player. OMG, what could I say to him as I called roll? I got to his name and told him (holding up two fingers intertwined) that Mrs. Birdwell, his teacher, and I were very good friends. His face lit up with that gap between his front teeth. From that day forward he was attached to me at the hip. Sometimes you had to go through him to get to me in class. Who was I to argue?

When a ninth grader came to my class for the second time with bruises on his neck and arms, I asked about them. He said he was playing around with some buddies. After class, some kids stayed and told me that the kid had a bad home life, and he was being initiated into a 'gang,' where a part of it was to go through a line and get beat up. Aha!

Next day, after class, I asked him to stay. "Listen to me. I know what is going on. If you ever come back into my class with any bruising, I will tell your parents, the school, and personally send you to a foreign prison where you will really get bruised up. You are worth something, you can be something, and you will work toward that. I have faith in you and trust you to do the right thing and I will always be here for you." Next day he told me he had dropped out of the group. Big relief.

Mid-70s, where the boys had haircuts like they were just inducted into the service: Whitewall. An unwritten rule of the theatre is you don't cut your hair before a show, as from the stage, you look rather bald. One night the catcher on the baseball team came 20 minutes early. I said he must have rushed home to shower and get here. He said yes. During a break, two other baseball players told me the coach said all of the team needed to get haircuts. The catcher told him that there was a play that weekend, and could he wait until Monday? No, he could not. The catcher quit and walked out.

After rehearsal we talked. I told him we could probably work something out, but he had to return to the team. He was a spectacular catcher. He said he would think about it.

Next morning before school, there was a knock on my door. Behold, the baseball coach, who asked me if I could get the team member to come back. I said he was going to, and the coach said he would allow them to wait for a haircut in the future. And, we really became good friends. His daughter was in drama, and the same haircut rules apply to the ladies, in case you were wondering.

Last one: One day during my planning period, I was going down the stairs and saw a student sitting there with his book open. I went to the office, came back and he was still there.

Second day. Same thing. I stopped and asked him why he was not in class. He said he had been put in the hall for being disruptive. When asked why, he said he was embarrassed when asked to read in class because he could not read well, and the kids mocked him. He was told to stand in the hall. To this day I never checked in with his teacher, and wondered why he was able to be on the steps for days. For the next two weeks, I spent my planning period (it's okay, some of us don't plan then) working with him and teaching him how to read. I can still remember coming around the corner going to the office one day and not seeing him there. He could make it in class. He worked so hard.

When a teacher has a class, they are teaching three different groups: The higher, middle and lower groups. We have to, more or less, teach down the center and try to include all.

After seeing a certain program used in another district, the head of the English department (the utterly brilliant and good, good friend), Deanne Wyatt, had the English classes divided into the three groups. I took the lower level.

On the first day, I asked them to raise their hands. "I see no one has a broken arm," I spouted, and told them to raise it no matter how times they have to, if they had a question.

Their book was a light teal. After the first class, they kind of hung around. I asked why and was told they did not want to carry around the book because everyone would know there were 'dummies.' I told them we could keep them in the room.

A moment: I wrote on the board "The house is yellow." I asked someone what the subject was. I got 'yellow' in response. Some kids giggled. I looked at one of them and asked them, since they were laughing, what the subject was?

"The." I corrected them and said there would be no laughing, just asking.

Once, when they were pushing back out of frustration, I told them we would take a vote. If you voted *Yes,* we would continue, and they would get better. If you chose the opposite, you could sit on one side of the classroom and do whatever, as long as you were quiet, and I would give you a 'D' and pass you on. I did say if they had a *No* vote, I would want them to give me a free soda when I stopped to get gas late at night in the gas station where they were working.

Got home and was sweating as I opened each vote. They were all *Yes.*

Lordy, the miles I travelled as hands kept popping up. One day there were no hands going up. OMG, I failed them. So, I walked up and down the aisles pretending I was bored and walking. There was not one mistake on the papers. With all the students being at the same level it was much easier to work at their level and a pace at which they would not feel intimidated. Nothing like struggling in a subject and having a bad reaction from other students. Happens all the time. They, in that environment, really blossomed.

Some parents protested the division, and the program was canceled after one year. What a shame. What a loss for the students who were thrown back into the lion's den of going down the middle.

My last year of teaching at Del City High School, a student came up after class and told me one of the boys had a gun in his back pocket. I had been around him and never saw it. He had baggy pants that hung halfway down his ass (great bit of fashion), and I had actually been behind him during class and noticed nothing. Called the office and he was apprehended as he was leaving school, and was suspended 3 weeks before graduation. He was going to sell the gun after school and, thankfully, it was not loaded.

I said I would retire when a student was in my class and uttered the dreaded words: 'You taught my father.' When it did happen, I felt like I was at least 95 years old.

New Year's Eve. 1969, Vietnam

We were in and out of the barracks, feeling no pain. There were like 15 or so of us standing in front of our barracks. Some soldiers were on the second floor balcony, hanging out windows. You know, the fun stuff.

I looked up to my left. Standing on the tiny balcony with a rifle was one drunk human. He shot up in the air. Since I had seen it, I did not move, but I swear when I looked around, I was standing by myself amongst sandals, beer bottles, food and the usual party favors. Literally, just me and the shooter, who got his comeuppance. I can still see it, me laughing, the others shouting obscenities at the reveler.

Hungry, getting a snack. Get yourself something, too.

I'm pretty good around blood, in that, if there was a fight at school I had to break up and there was blood, I was fine. Vietnam was a different matter. Our MSGT was being sent home, and we went to the hospital barracks to say goodbye. Entered and had to turn left to go down the hall. There were gurneys lining both sides of the hall, and it was difficult to walk because of doctors and nurses trying to help.

One soldier was on a gurney, naked except for a sheet draped over his groin. Sticking out of several parts of his body was shrapnel and blood all over. As I started to pass, he took my hand and pleaded, 'Please help me." I tried to offer some kind words and walked out. I said goodbye to the MSGT outside as he waved from a second story window. I can still see it, but could not handle it.

You know how they ask me to do things. Some guy (coming in from duty in the field) was in the shower for two hours. I went in, pretending to do something, and asked if he was okay. He smiled. He was, and this was his first hot shower in six months.

Okay, I do hereby note I am not a camping kind of guy. Like the old saying, "If there is a hotel nearby, I'm one happy camper." Not the case during basic training at good ole' Ft. Bliss in hot, hot Texas. We were going out for the night after a day of this, to make us killing machines.

You had one half of a tent, your partner had the other. Set it up. I looked over and saw quite the sight. This guy had dug out like 2 inches of soil in the shape of a yard at a house in front of his tent. What the...? He said it was his 'patio' and he would invite some of us over later for drinks.

We were at attention as the Lieutenant walked down the row, looking right and left. He saw the 'patio', took one more step, and without looking around or turning, took one step back and turned to the soldier who was now not so sure about the drinks after, I am thinking.

"Soldier, what is that?" Pause.

"It's a...a patio, Sir."

"Patio?"

In what was becoming a very soft voice, "Yes, Sir...it's a....it's a patio." It was so quiet you could hear a fish fart in a bowl. The Earth almost stopped spinning. Okay, enough.

Lieutenant stood there, looking down, turned and walked on. The soldier gulped and wiped the sweat off of his face, "I'm glad he didn't ask me about the playroom downstairs."

That night, what kept us awake was not critters that might attack or eat us. It was some damn scorpions going up one side of our tent and sliding down the other. All night play time for them.

Which three words would you choose for which you would like to be remembered?

Having trouble sleeping? Well, this isn't something to help you sleep, but stay up wondering: Who invented words? Who looked up and said, "Sky." Or, "Hey, Friend, doesn't that look like grass?" And, then to have to put them together to make sentences (Much less diagram them). All the discussions of what to call what. For example, imagine looking at your hand and calling it a termite. Or, "I'm going to brush my tibia."

Choosing numbers! Get back to me.

PS: And all those languages. *Cherche les/Que da/Impara una lingua.*

Four of us from the dorm at college decided to make a jaunt to Dallas. For fun, we went to an XXX movie. Never did in Oklahoma. What we liked to do when watching a video was to turn down the volume and make up our own dialogue. After a few beers we were pretty darn funny. We paid and I was the last in. Not many people there, or what we could tell in the dark. We sat in the front row ready to begin our dialogue.

The lights suddenly came on, illuminating the whole place, and the manager, followed by a police officer, walked right up to us. The manager pointed at me and said, "He robbed us." The cashier came running down the aisle and said it was not me, but the man behind me. Confusion, because the robber and I both wore red sweaters. All I could see in front of my eyes was the headline in an Oklahoma newspaper (not to mention world-wide), "Oklahoma teacher robs porno movie in Dallas." Suddenly the XXX's became OOO's, and we left. One guy in a red sweater was sweating.

My mother's sister Martha, and her husband, Duane, were grade school sweethearts. Ahhh. They were so much fun. Whereas my mother could be a little stuffy, Martha and Duane were game for anything. For a time they lived in Shiprock, New Mexico. There was a two-lane highway from there to Farmington. Coming back from a trip with Duane, he asked me if I wanted to drive? Hello! Who cared if I was 15, I could drive. Off we went from Farmington to Shiprock, one long, straight road with nary a stoplight, sign, or distraction. For a short while he slept.

Ironically, when he woke up, I was getting ready to pass an old pickup truck with something crammed in the back. I passed it. My uncle, in an easy tone noted, "Buddy, you came in a little too fast after you passed the truck." I looked in the rearview mirror to see the pickup going down a small embankment with items bouncing out of the truck. Yikes! Give more room. Duly noted.

Martha and Duane invited two friends over for dinner. It was the 50s. In the door walked the most beautiful couple I had ever seen. Both looked like models: He was blond (you know the rest), and she was this breathtaking Native American in the traditional dress. While we ate, I kept sneaking glances at them. They were smiling all the time, and just radiated love for each other.

After they left, of course, I mentioned their striking looks and how I could not take my eyes off his wife. Martha told me the couple had come from the Midwest to make a life in New Mexico. When they got married, there was trouble in their little town with harassment, nasty signs in the yard, and negative comments as they passed. He was white and she was black. By moving to New Mexico, and with her skin tone, they were able to enjoy a wonderful life.

Back in Oklahoma, Martha and Duane bought some land and had animals, most of which thought they were lap dogs. One frisky 'child' was Nibbles, the goat. His name says it all. He would walk to the lake with you, off the leash, which was close. He wasn't so cute when I walked out, and the little bugger was on my car hood eating some leaves from a tree I parked under to get out of the sun.

The aunt and uncle from Kansas City had come to visit Oklahoma and go to Martha and Duane's for lunch and chit-chat. Nibbles was around sniffing everyone and sometimes getting pushed away. Here we go with another aunt from Kansas City laugh-fest. Out she came with her paper plate of food, walked to a folding mesh chair, and quite promptly fell through, her bottom hitting the ground and her feet flying up, so she looked like a smashed sandwich. Nibbles must have thought it would be fun to do just that with the mesh chair. Told you had I to laugh at such events. Mother pushed me and said go away.

* * * * * * * * * * * * * * * * * * *

At the end of the school year, schools have an evening of honoring students for all types of things. The auditorium is packed. Teachers, staff and whomever, sat on the stage in two rows divided so the podium did not block anyone. I was on the second row. Desa Dawson, who taught Spanish, was giving the award for the best Spanish student.

About that time, I noticed a spider on the arm of the vacant chair in front of me. It sat on the edge. Desa talked. Deanne, sitting next to me, gently touched my arm and pointed to the creepy crawler. I whispered I saw it. Desa began to speak in Spanish. The spider began to slowly descend from the arm. What to do? For some reason, halfway down it started swinging left to right. My head did, too. I've got it! As the spider began to crawl back up the string, I slowly took off my shoe. I would lean forward and gently smack it while Desa was talking.

I raised my shoe and leaned forward. In that split second Desa stopped talking to take a breath. My shoe hitting the arm of the chair echoed in the auditorium. Desa jumped and turned to me, glaring. I had my shoe up in the air from swatting as she turned. The audience began to laugh. Afterwards, I tried to explain what happened and Deanne backed me up. Desa was justifiably upset. But, she became even more upset when I followed her with my awards and started speaking some made-up language for a few seconds. Audience: 10; Desa: 9; Chuck: ZERO.

When I moved to Del City High School a few years later, she was there. We had been friends at Carl Albert and had a good laugh at the infamous spider episode.

You are driving late at night through a small town. You hit someone and kill them. If you knew you would never be caught, would you stay or go?

The best laid plans, and all that jazz. A friend and I went to Six Flags in Texas. One of the attractions we decided to try was rowing a canoe over a body of water. Rowing is not as easy as it is made out to be. So, off we go, all eight or so of us. As we begin to huff and puff and row in the hot summer sun, our Adonis guide asks us to keep rowing when some let up a little. He, meanwhile, leans off the canoe front getting a tan on an already bronzed body that only has on some sort of loin cloth with a speedo under it.

The "crew" begins to get a little irritated as he narrates something none of us remember. We canoe captives notice another canoe coming toward us. They, too, are sweaty and a little more than hot because of their situation, which is the same as ours. We look at each other in the canoe and begin to row like there is no tomorrow. Closer. Closer. Row, Row. Row your boat. Splat! There is nothing quite like the sound of two Adonis bodies crashing together as they both fall in the water. Row, Row, Row your boat. For some reason, (insert chuckle here), both of them were upset upon reentering our domain. Ours, as we gleefully row away, chastises us for not letting him know. We tell him we did not see the other boat because we were soooo busy rowing. Fun trip!

* * * * * * * * * * * * * * * * * *

MSGT Renta, at Ft. Lewis, was sent to Tan Son Nhut Air Base in the vacation mecca of Viet Nam. When I found out I was going, I wrote him, and he said he would make a spot for me.

Ta Da! I board the plane, a luxury liner, and I take my seat in first class. (My ass). There was a group of oldies and newbies on the way in a commercial jet. As we fly, I imagine the fun of seeing MSGT Renta, the 'fun' I'll have. A slight bump with the plane.

I bet I am going to love being on the base. Second, third and fourth bump. Hmmm, getting a little rough.

As the plane begins to bank to the left, the pilot tells everyone to be seated and fasten their seat belts. Tell that to all the men in the aisle who have to do their business or throw up. We turn and head for Saigon because of a monsoon. What??!! We have to go to Tan Son Nhut. MGST Renta is waiting for me. The wheels touch down in Saigon. Good-bye, better times at TSN.

The oldies are pretty happy as we descend, discussing which bar they will go to and the pretty girls they will find. The newbies are turning pale at the turbulence and thoughts of maybe going down in a hurricane before we ever get there. Land.

Pilot: "Be sure you run in a zig zag bent over as you run to the pavilion." Let me tell you, I stepped out of the plane (hearing rifles/something being shot in the distance), blinked, and this newbie was under the pavilion.

One day at work I noticed one of the Vietnamese women cleaning up the building, rubbing a smooth rock on her forearm. There was already one bruise there. I asked my co-worker what she was doing, and was told to get rid of a pain, they rub a smooth rock over the spot and it 'goes away.' Goes away? Of course, it goes away, because they just rubbed a new pain to stop the old pain. Tried it once. It works, all right, but damn, my arm was bruised, and it hurt. I had to try it, so don't judge.

Remember cassette tapes? I have CD's and DVD's that, although I took excellent care of them, have scratches that really irritate me. However, I have cassette tapes that are at least 25 years old that play without a problem. And, I did not treat them any better than those mentioned above. Love those old tapes.

I wear a loose T-Shirt when I sleep. I don't like my shoulders to get cold. What I wear below is none of your business.

Imagine this: You have come back from Vietnam. For Pete's sake—Vietnam—and you are sitting in a chair being processed, and are told you will be assigned to a National Guard unit. Are you fucking kidding me?! I politely declined and said I would go to Canada first. I had no intention of going on weekend retreats. I was not assigned a unit. By-the-by, I did have an ex-friend who did go to Canada, and came home, knocked on my door to say hello and chat. I did not let him in, but wished him luck, telling him I did not appreciate his going to Canada while there was turmoil, and then coming home to enjoy the fruits of labor actual soldiers made on his behalf. I closed the door.

Jackpot! There were 1,200 grade school students at the Criterion Theatre in OKC to watch some movie. At the end they were going to give away a Schwinn bicycle. We had been given tickets, and I memorized the number, and put it in my pocket. The announcer starts calling out the numbers. They sounded familiar. Wait! That is my ticket number. I reached into my coat pocket. No ticket. I frantically started looking around on the floor, my jeans, my shoes, and several seats to my right and left. Friends are helping. The announcer says since there is no response, he will call the second number. The student got a brand new, shiny Schwinn bike. I actually cried a little on the bus on the way home. Everyone was trying to comfort poor Buddy. Got home and relayed the news to my parents, who were so sympathetic. Went to my room, took off my coat, and sat on the bed holding it. I reached into my right pocket. What the...? There was a hole. I reached in and pulled the winning ticket. Cried all over again. That was in November. Come Christmas morning I walked into the living room to see the same bike and color by the tree. One of the best Christmas presents ever. Glad I didn't run away, after all, when I was a young pup.

Isn't it funny how many of us have trouble with the most minimal of tasks? For the life of me I can't fold those darn windscreen thing-a-ma-bobs. I turn them every which way but loose. I've broken a few along the way. The easy solution is to throw the damn things in the back seat until further needed. When I actually folded one correctly for the first time, I felt like Albert Einstein.

Not a gambler. Been to Vegas several times and stayed away from the one-armed bandits. However, one time my friend wanted to do the slot machines. Bored, I walked around and saw a line of machines not in use. Being away from the crowd appealed to me. Down I sat. After putting in a few quarters I heard a strange sound. Several tokens began to fall out. Okay, so I made a few bucks. Boring. Of course, the man who does not like slot machines puts in a quarter. Bingo! More tokens.

Like every three out of five times I put in a quarter, the tokens would fall. An employee actually gave me a bucket. I was not looking around, just putting in the quarters. Bingo! I thought enough is enough, and decided to cash in. There were like twelve people standing around me. The slot machine had made so much noise each time, it sounded like a constant ringing. I could not get off of my chair as so many were trying to get my seat. I really fought to get out. Gave the bucket to the employee and got back over $600. I still hate losing money and rarely played, or if I did, it was a $5 limit.

The bathroom door on a plane would not stay shut while I stood and did my business. Try that while trying to put a foot at the door to keep it closed. Finished. When I came out, two stewardesses sat outside the door at the back of the plane. "You didn't hear us out here, did you?" I said no and she said, "Good, because we heard everything out here. Sounded like Niagara Falls." They looked at each other and smiled. I was so naïve back then. Nowadays I could have sued and owned the airline, for comparing me, a poor customer who really had to go, to Niagara Falls. What a compliment.

I think it's odd some cell phones won't let you cuss, but send all types of asterisks or whatever. Now, I have been known to have a mouth like a drunken sailor (as Grandpa would say), so it would disturb me if my colorful language was not transmitted correctly. Just a fact, unfortunately: I cuss so much it's like a second language to me and thankfully, luckily, my friends accept it. I've tried to curb it, but it just doesn't last long. It is not my fault that some of my friends have found my colorful language catching. The first time I would hear them use such a word I would have to stifle a laugh. Enough of the etiquette lesson.

Remember Jiffy Pop? (Google) Not a good thing to have one in the college dorm on a hotplate (banned) that does not pop correctly. Had it going and noticed some smoke. The tin foil cover was not rising, and the kernels were burning. We quickly opened the windows as we heard some popping. The room was engulfed in smoke. Knock on the door. I opened it to see the floor counselor standing there.

I was surrounded by smoke which wafted out the door, into his face and into the hall. "Yes? Is there a problem?" I asked. He stepped in a few steps, waving the smoke from his face. "Get rid of this. Now." I put the container outside on the ledge, smoke still pouring out. Hot plate retired.

The same goes for a tiny lizard my roommate had. One night I heard scratching. We looked in his glass aquarium. No tiny lizard. Looked everywhere. Not to be found. The next night I woke up to hear my roomie screaming. I turned on the light and he is batting the air. The lizard, hiding under a closet runner, had come out and climbed on his face. Poor thing ran back to its hiding place, never to be seen again. Never smelled anything bad, so I assume he took up quarters elsewhere.

A good thing was when a pizza establishment in OKC held a contest. The winning entry of how much you loved Shotgun Sam's Pizza, would get a pizza party for 100. Yep, I won. Invited everyone I knew. In case you are wondering, I wrote a funny (big surprise) poem. My picture was in the CSC newspaper. When I heard my name called out on the radio as the winner, I went to the lobby and called the station, and was immediately put on the air. Suddenly, the lobby had like 20 people asking me to invite them. That was in East Hall, a newly built dorm. I was in room 323, I think or something in the 300's.

Brad Pitt is from Oklahoma, as am I. We were having lunch the other day. Sorry, I meant Reba McEntire. Or was it Garth Brooks? I never had lunch with any of them. Maybe once this book comes out...

If only the delicious, mouth-watering items on the box looked like that when it was cooked.

At more than one party, when people heard I taught English would say, "Oh, no, now don't be correcting my English." My usual reply was, "I don't give a rat's ass how you speak. I'm here to eat and drink. Go away, you're bothering me." Okay, it did not go down like that. I was very nice and said I was here to have a good time, too. That, of course, made me follow them around to see why they were worried.

November 22, 1963, was opening night at CSU for the play, "The Cave Dwellers," a play about a group of misfits. I played The King, a celebrated clown. Another cast member and I walked in the TV room at the dorm, and saw like 25 people around the TV. As I walked to the staircase I asked what was going on.

"The President has been shot in Dallas." Some joke. Up we went and got things we needed for the play and came back down. Group was still glued to the set. I moved in. Like everyone in that situation, my mind went numb. What? How did this happen?

The play was cancelled that night. We 'opened' the next night. I had a line where I stand in the double doors, facing away from the audience and bellow a line that went something like, "Enough. Enough violence." I froze because the audience broke into applause that lasted several seconds.

My costume was quite unique, and I had on old age makeup. A friend who worked for the school paper happened to be there and asked to take my picture. I was tired, a little grumpy, and not wanting my picture taken. Can you imagine an actor saying that? He was so nice I had to say yes, BUT only one picture, I advised.

Click. The picture turned out so perfect that the fringe on my scarf was not blurred, and he submitted it to the state newspaper where it won his division, and it got him a job at the paper. I still look at a picture I did not want taken that is perfect in every way. You can look for it in my coffee table book that will come out in 2032.

Oh, the language barrier. Why was I not fluent in at least five languages? Boarding in Russia, Linda and I were pulled aside. Luckily, that did not happen often. Young man opened my suitcase and looked. He took out a small can of hair spray and looked, really looked it over. He looked at his friend. To help, I held my hand up by my head and made a spray sound. Young man looked totally confused. I repeated the gesture, but this time I lifted my combover and made a PSSST sound. No expression. His friend laughed, put the can back in my luggage and off we went. It's hard, let me tell you, to try and lift a combover that is sprayed and feels like it has Crazy Glue on it. But mission accomplished.

* * * * * * * * * * * * * * * * * * * *

While going to college, I worked at John A. Brown's, an upscale department store that had all types of wonderful things. One was Mrs. Brown herself. A short, plump woman who had her driver drop her off a block from the store for fear of being kidnapped. She wore a turban because she had thinning hair.

The second time I met her (wiggling in my chair, remembering this one) was on the elevator. I was hired to run the elevators. The old, fun kind where you make it run and stop on a dime at the correct floor. I was told by Linda (Not that one), who was over the ten of us, that if Mrs. Brown got on, take her directly to the third floor where her office was, and do not stop on any floor. The store was having one of their big sales and it was packed.

Into the basement came Mrs. Brown with a soft greeting. I froze. I stopped on the first floor and opened the door. I see this turban being shoved to the back corner. I should be fired about 3 minutes from now when she gets off. Second floor. Third floor. Mrs. Brown is the last off. She stops by me with a sweet, "I like to ride with the customers...sometimes. Don't let it happen again." And off she went. The first time we met was on a snowy February day. We were told to never speak to her. Only problem was I did not know who she was. The elevator door opened and Linda, who was training me, came to attention. The woman said how much she enjoyed the snow. I said the same, and we talked about snow to the third floor.

Door opened, she stopped and turned to me with a, "It was nice chatting with you." Only after Linda nearly fainted did she tell me it was THE Mrs. Brown. And I talked to her. In training and fired all in the same day. No such fate met me.

Last time I saw her was after hours. I took her from one floor to another so she could attend a board meeting. She did not have her turban on, but had had her hair done. As she walked away, I just had to say, "Mrs.

Brown?" She turned. "You look so pretty." She said thank you with a smile, and off she went.

Like with any job, one can get bored. One can even have fun in the elevator. If, in your elevator, you put your head against the wall, you can see into the elevator beside you. Or at least the operator and any person standing by the front wall. I turned off my lights in the elevator in the basement. As their door closed I made a ghostly, "Ooooo." Stopped on first floor. They continued to the second floor where I let out another wail. Their conversation was as follows:

"What was that?"

"What?"

"That Oooooo."

"What Oooo?"

Elevator operator is biting his lip. I insert another wail.

"That Oooo."

"Is that a ghost? (To operator) Did you hear that Oooo?"

"No, Ma'am.'

"I want out. This elevator is haunted."

Oh, the fun ghostly adventures.

I'm glad I never gave anyone a heart attack. On the Main Street side of the store, the elevators were the old-fashioned ones that you controlled at all times. On the Park Avenue side there were newer elevators where you pull the lever down, which starts the elevator, and you can take your hand off after ten seconds. However, if you push the lever down and the elevator starts to move and you take your hand off, the elevator shudders and shakes and stops. Mutters of terror for a few seconds before I apologize and off we go. I'm not sure where I got this streak. From Charlie, being the middle child, or I just had a mean streak. Your choice.

I was out taking my usual walk in the apartment complex where I live. I always have my earbuds in, hat on, and sunglasses. When I was almost back at my humble abode, I bent down to pick up a piece of mail I had dropped, and suddenly my vision was off. One side seemed perfect, the other off kilter. I stepped into the apartment, thinking I was on my way to a mini stroke (long before my real one), and realized that when I bent over, one of the lens had fallen out, and I did not notice it. Crisis averted. Went out to get and replace the lens.

I don't think I am the only person in the world who gets frustrated when asked to answer at least twenty prompts before you actually speak to a person. When I look at all the numbers I had to enter it looks like the German war debt.

Any-who, we can all relate to: "This conversation may be recorded for quality assurance." What the hell is that? I actually asked someone what it meant. I got some stumbling, some mutter and finally they did not know the exact meaning. Or, you give the recorded phantom all the information, only to talk to a person who asks, "May I have...?" and it's all the information you already told the robot. Sheesh. I had to ask why I am repeating myself and they say it did not transfer. OR, you give the information only to be told, "I'll have to transfer you to another department, where the first question is "May I have....?" My idea of hell is have these people call and go through it all. My mom got so mad at dad because when he got a robo call (Not called those then), he would keep them on the line for about 15-20 minutes asking questions. Then he would say no, thank you, and hang up.

I am thankful for my genes. At least 40 years ago I saw an article commenting on all the beauty products out there that basically don't do much. It stated that if you want to see what you are going to look like later in life, look at your parents and grandparents. Thank the Gene Gods that my family did not look their age. When I was teaching, inevitably some students would ask my age. I would tell them. They asked to see my driver's license, which I don't carry. It's in the glove compartment. They would look at one another and say, "I told you he would lie." A young clerk asked for my ID when I went to get beer. She gasped and said she was sorry, but she thought I was not of age. I was 25.

Which, if either, bothers you most: take-off or landing? Neither for me, until I saw videos of a couple of planes that crashed 40 seconds after take-off. So, for the next few flights I could breathe a sigh of relief after that 40 second count down.

Now mid-air is an entirely different story. Dropped Linda off in good ole' St. Louis on the way to OKC. The flight is an hour and some change. About 30 minutes into the flight, the pilot came on and said we had to return to St. Louis. That was it. No biggie. That is until we started to land, and I looked out the window to see ambulances, fire trucks, and the police lined up by the runway. Landed with no problem and I never did hear what almost killed us at 25,000 feet, only to drop from the sky and burn up, so we all looked like burnt shish kabobs in several pieces spread over at least four counties. Enough about that flight.

I love Lyn Cramer, this talented actor, performer and teacher. She was one of the choreographers for the Yuletide Festival at the Civic Center, under Maestro Joel Levine. After school, I went to OCU for rehearsal. There she sat, watching another number being staged in which she was not involved. I sat by her and hugged her. She gently pushed me away and said I needed to stay away as she was not feeling well. I said I did not get sick and stayed by her. She was called to stage the next number. Up she jumped as if she had found the fountain of youth and worked on the number, and then came back and sank on a step. I never forgot that moment and did the same for the rest of my life and career. Hugs, Lyn.

The same cannot be said for the stewardess on the plane when we finally left Vietnam. We were supposed to leave the night before, but the end of the runway had been bombed. (Someone get me a bazooka and I'll handle this!). The plane was extremely hot, even after sitting all night. The men were elated to be leaving and were in a party mood. Not drinking, but laughing and sharing stories about their adventures.

The stewardess, walking up and down the aisle before take-off, was inundated with playful cat calls (nothing out of line. Just happy to see a female not dressed in military gear). She scoffed them all and became so rude that the men stopped talking to her. She was abrupt about no service until we were in the air. They could not get up and roam around before take-off and stuff like that. Okay, you know me well enough by now in this narrative that, as she walked down the aisle, snapping at some soldiers, I put my arm across the aisle on the other seat and she ran into it and bent over a little because she was moving so fast. The one-sided conversation went something like this: "I know you might be having a bad day. You might be tired. You might be ready to get back to the states, too, but you are here to serve men who have been in Vietnam fighting for you, your family, and all of the United States, and you need to give them the kindness, respect and service they deserve." As she apologized, the men around us broke into applause.

When we stepped out of the plane in the good ole' USA the air smelled so sweet. I was only there for six months (would never have gone had they honored my early out for college, but that's another story), but those there longer stood on the tarmac, and just like you saw in all those pictures and newsreels, got on their knees and kissed the tarmac. So many were not given that opportunity.

I never was a cook. Oh, there were dishes I used to make, but with two jobs, it was so easy to pop something into the microwave. A friend from college stayed overnight and the next morning we thought of pancakes, but there was no mix. Granny came in the kitchen and told us she would make pancakes. We informed her there was no mix. She said she did not need a mix and proceeded to make actual pancakes from scratch. In awe, we both watched, and he told everybody back at the dorm the feat she had accomplished without a box of mix.

Which brings me to: I see articles in magazines which show famous people and dishes they make (and you can make at home. Yikes!) One of them had eleven ingredients, while the other had 9. I admire anyone who would buy all of those ingredients and actually make the time to cook them. I would be a great guest if you invited me over to partake.

Here's one for you. After 41 years at the Jewel Box, we had our number of complaints. The only one that amazed me was infidelity or implied infidelity in a play. Not all, but some people got in a snit when the subject was done (not actually XXX done), suggested, or alluded to. When someone would call or write about it, I always had the same reply: You're complaining about infidelity. Yes. What would you say if some men were given poison and died and were buried in a cellar, never to be heard from again? That's terrible. Or should a drunk woman run an orphanage? Never. What would your response be to two star-crossed lovers from rival gangs who slept together? That is unacceptable. (The big finish) Then I'm confused as to why you didn't call when we did 'Arsenic and Old Lace', 'Annie', and 'West Side Story", to name a few. I see your point. Thank you for calling. (And why does that subject bother you so much???)

When people/students would ask me why take Speech and Drama, I always had the same reply: You might be nervous, but you will look better doing it.

A project I gave to students every year (feel to try this yourself), was to go to a party and do the following:

1. Concentrate on the person to whom you are speaking.

2. Ask them all types of questions about themselves.

3. If they ask you a question, answer, and then return talking about them.

At the end of the night you will find those people telling everyone how wonderful you were, and they will know very little about you, because, we all like to talk about our favorite subject: Ourselves.

The number one fear of the American public is not death or dying, but public speaking. Some say to imagine them all naked while you speak and that will change how you feel. For me, the only feeling would be nausea.

So, that goes with acting. Getting in front of people and showing them a character that is not yourself, helps actors to 'hide' in a character, which makes it easier for some actors. The number one question I aways get is, "How do they remember all those lines?" to which I reply, "After working on a play for four weeks I would hope they remember their lines, like you remembering all the information you have in the directory in your mind."

That said, it also means you can 'go up' or forget a line. As professional and brilliant as I am as an actor, I have committed that sin. If you are lucky, the person who gets a blank stare can jump in and work it so they say your line and combine it with theirs. If they can't react, you are screwed, and that 5 second delay until someone can cover, seems like it was at the very least 30 seconds.

Different actors work different ways. Some need lots of discussion and some take off and run with it and some do the 'method' thing and become the character on and offstage type of thing. Paul Rudd has a quote I love: "I hear people talk about 'the craft' and I think, you are so full of shit." Priceless.

Example: working on "One Flew Over the Cuckoo's Nest" and the actress playing Nurse Ratchet wanted to talk about her character. Having directed for a number of years, I have grown to know how to discuss 'the method.' (I have nothing against it. Whatever works for you). She said she was having trouble knowing how Ratchet became like she was. So, off we went. I told her, perhaps, as a child, she tore wings off of butterflies and hid a deep resentment for people in general. She said she got it and off she went. My stage manager pulled a Rudd on me and said, 'You are so full of shit.' I agreed, but Nurse Ratchet was born.

The cast had to laugh at the girl playing Susy in "Wait Until Dark" at the high school, because when she had to scream in terror, out came a flat sort of comic squeak. We talked and she could not get it. During a break I asked one of the janitors, working at night, who was a wrestler and in a class of mine, if he would grab her when she walked from the auditorium to the school. He was to grab her and put her on the ground. The cast and I peeked out the auditorium door as he jumped out from around the corner and grabbed her. Out came this blood-curdling scream as he gently put her on the ground. As he held her down, he looked toward the door and asked, "Was that alright, Mr. Tweed?" She looked at me, threw him off and came running after me, calling me some names only sailors know, and for real, chased me around the auditorium for a few rounds.

Judges from a theatre group went to see high school shows and would choose three to perform downtown OKC. From eleven shows, we were lucky to be chosen, and the actress playing Susy won Best Actress (Judges noting her scream was terrifying).

In that same show was an actor playing Mike, his first show. After being 'stabbed,' he was supposed to fall down the six steps to the bottom, face first. We talked about how to fall. He said he got it. He got 'stabbed' from behind, fell to his knees and bounced down the steps on his front, head bouncing off of the steps until he crashed at the bottom of the stairs. The actor who had 'stabbed' him came running down the steps, the crew came out and I ran from the middle of the auditorium and surrounded what we thought was now a dead body. He rolled over and smiled with, "How was that?" When we performed for the school and the night audiences, they always gasped in horror.

Last one: An actor was to walk to the side of the stage and stick his hand by the curtain pulley. He shoved his hand in and froze, then went on with the play, holding his finger. The phone rang at the back of the auditorium, and I was told he had cut his finger and there was blood everywhere and the leading lady said she would throw up, pass out, or die if she had to go on. I went backstage and said the show must go on and shoved her onstage. When the play ended, I went on stage to see blood on the desk, in the typewriter keys as he had to type something, on the floor, and on him. While cleaning up his wound, a woman came up and pushed us all aside and took over. Before I could speak, she said, 'I'm his mother and a nurse.'

God love actors who can bravely carry on.

It takes quite a person to stand up for the underdog. I told my classes that a bully was a tiny, insecure mouse who picked on others to feel better about themselves, when they don't actually feel good about themselves.

This goes with that. My parents knew the principal, vice-principal and superintendent. So, they were somewhat surprised when the VP of the junior high asked them to come up, regarding my younger brother. He had not said anything at dinner that night, so they were confused. The VP told them my brother had held a student up against the lockers after, for the third time, he had run by and flicked one of my brother's friends hearing aids, and brother told him what would happen to him if he ever did it again. VP said they need to talk to him about how to handle such offenses, and (sidebar), he would not be punished.

Although I was not around bullies in school, something about seeing more than one bully gang up on one person because they feel there is safety in numbers, made my blood boil, as you might have guessed from this work of art.

I try to be patient in situations, but sometimes I can't help it. Big surprise! After 9/11, I was going through the line at an airport, and five people behind this man started yelling his phone was not in the bin. The worker said it had to be somewhere close if he put it in. She suggested looking around for some of his items, but he would not be placated. "Where is my phone? I'm going to sue." The next bin out had his phone in it.

The worker gave him his phone. He kept going. Well, Tweed had had it.

"Move it!" I snapped. "You got your phone, and we want to get through this line." He grumbled, grabbed his phone and left. Some passengers thanked me, and I thought, "Why didn't you say something?" I know it's because people do not want to get in a fight or whatever.

Half-way up the Statue of Liberty, she started to gently shake. We later found out a quick storm had come through. When we got down there were some broken tree branches. With the gentle shaking, a woman at the top starts moaning that the statue was shaking and we will all be killed. People tried to calm her down, but to no avail. Tweed: "Move it." Echoing down the stairs to me was, "Who said that?"

"Doesn't matter. Move!" She did. I am just exhausted helping people.

What would you do if, at a department store, you saw a six-year-old boy climbing on a platform with a store dummy held up by fishing line?

I looked around. No mom I could see. He moved up and grabbed the leg of the mannequin. Oh, boy, he is about to fall. I told him to get down. Mom came flying over telling me I should not discipline her son. I told her what she missed, and I would do it again. His head was down as they walked off with mom reading him the riot act.

That age again. Sixth in line at the post office where there are two glass doors to enter, with curtains that were pulled back. A little bugger kept jerking on the cord to make the curtains jump as people came in. The older ones kind of scared me as they reacted. On the fourth jerk, I told him to stop. He froze and slowly moved toward a person. I could not wait to see who the culprit was. It was his grandmother in front of me. He stood in front of her and, when he peeked around once, I bent over, made a fist, and showed my snarl. See. I am just exhausted.

There are many times I am able not to do the afore mentioned. Not the case when I visited a former student who had a toddler. They had a puppy and the little girl, her hair in dog ears (important later), went over to the puppy and grabbed his ears and jerked him up a foot or so. I looked at the student, and he had those eyes that begged me to let it go. I did. She went over to the VCR and tried to shove a tape in the wrong way. Nothing said or done. I can handle this.

So proud of myself. However, when she went back over to the dog and pulled his ears up, Chuck got up, grabbed her by her dog ears and pulled her up. "How do you like it? It hurts, doesn't it? It hurts the dog, too. Don't do it again." The child ran to mommy and cried. No, I did not pull hard, so you can back down on the violence of it all.

As I left. I apologized to them, but told them that was not acceptable. They said they agreed. For some reason, for a few months after, she would run and hide behind mommy or daddy when Chuck, the dog-ear-puller, came over. Be afraid. Be very afraid.

Has this ever happened to you? Many moons ago a friend from college went to the funeral of a colleague from work. He arrived just as it started. He got out the Kleenex. A few sentences in the speaker said, "We are here to celebrate the life of Jane Doe. (Not her name, of course.) The friend looked up. What? He was here for the funeral of Suzy Smith (not actual, either). What to do?

He sat through the funeral, and instead of walking by the casket of the unknown body, he went toward the entrance to get out. The man at the door said he would have to exit by the side door with everyone else. He said no and passed by and stood with the people awaiting entrance. Two little old ladies came over, and quite loudly, asked him what he was doing. 'Are you one of those funeral hoppers who goes from funeral to funeral and cries?" He sputtered and said he knew Suzy, but they scoffed and left him. I must admit it was hard to sit there and show compassion while inside I was laughing my ass off.

At the end of the school year, we all meet at a school auditorium where several people are recognized. When it came time for the retired teachers to be recognized, they lined up on one side and walked across the stage. I thought there is no way in hell I am not going out without a bang. When they called my name (down to the T's), I was not in line. However, when Dr. Steele, the Superintendent, started to move on, I marched down the aisle, throwing candy to the crowd. Everyone turned, laughed, and applauded.

Dr. Steele, God love her, froze. (Everyone freezes in my snippets). I said a few words, and exited the other aisle, throwing candy.

That summer, when I was out with friends to eat, some man said, "Excuse me." He stood up and had on a Carl Albert High School coach's shirt. "Weren't you the man who threw candy during the retirement part of the assembly?" I told him yes, and he said people were still talking about it, as it had never been done before. Or since, I might add.

I applaud the weather people who cover all that goes on with Oklahoma weather. They stay on for hours and hours letting us know it's raining. The weather person stands there with 2-3 live shots around the state. They are asked what is going on where they are. "It's really coming down, Joe Bob. You can see the heavy rain making it hard to drive." Thank you, and what's going on where you are, Dale Bob?" "It's really coming down, Joe Bob. You can see the heavy rain making it hard to drive." Kudos to them for keeping the state informed when some actual bad weather happens. Sometimes, I wish they would hold off for a while so we can watch our shows. This is not a slam to any channel on the Oklahoma weather. I have to move on because it's really coming down, Rob Bob.

I loved hearing stories from grandpa, but have my own to tell about the "good ole days." For example, when I first enrolled at Central State College in 1916, and got to school by horse and buggy, it was a two-lane highway with no lights until you got into Edmond proper.

Also, it was an outrageous fifteen cents to call the city from Edmond. Well, Buddy had no money, so he was going to call home collect. My visiting great grandmother, whom I adored, answered. The operator asked if she would accept a collect call. No, she would not. I started begging for her to take the call. I could hear the operator snickering as we went back and forth with, I will pay you when I come home this weekend. This is important. Finally, giggling, the operator, after about 30 seconds of this, said she would have to disconnect us if Granny would not accept. Finally, she agreed, and still giggling, connected us.

Granny Nick stayed with one daughter for six months, then did the same with the other. Granny Madden in OKC, and Aunt Maggie (yes, that one), in Kansas City.

One night I was watching TV in my bedroom and kept running down for drinks and snacks. I heard her snap her fingers as I bounded up like four steps. In a hurry to get back, I asked what she wanted.

With a stern face she said, "You wet that bed and I'll blister you." I laughed all the way upstairs. I keep saying, although there were some difficult times, I felt loved and appreciated with a charmed life. Of course, one does not realize it until many years later.

In New York City in the NBC building lobby, I heard some buzzing going on. I looked, and running, like he did in the car commercial, was O.J. Simpson, but to an elevator. As he passed me, he smiled, "Sorry I can't stop. I'm in a hurry."

At Ft. Lewis, we were called out for PT. We were standing shoulder-to-shoulder when the Sgt told us to do jumping jacks. Really? Side-by-side jumping jacks? Some laughter from the guys.

"Uh, Sgt?"

"Yes?"

"For the jumping jacks", I suggested, "might we take one step to our right, arm's length?" He agreed.

* * * * * * * * * * * * * * * * * *

I will be your tour guide for the next few pages.

To me, it doesn't matter where you go as long as you enjoy it. When people say they are only going to...(fill in the blank), I tell them at least they are getting away and enjoy.

 1. Martha and Duane took Susy and me to Mesa Verde National Park in Colorado when we were teenagers. The history, and the scope of the largest cliff dwelling in North America, boggles the eyes and mind. You can go in and crawl around through tiny tunnels. Well, this skinny boy made a turn and vowed he could wiggle through. Not! After Sis asked for some help to get the 'Triangle' out of the tunnel, I was pulled, pushed and prodded to the exit. It's one of those trips I can still see when I close my eyes.

 2. Mt. Ranier in Washington state was always stunning to look at. Even more fun was to have soldiers come into the Overseas Replacement Station, where I was assigned, and see low-lying clouds—only to wake

up and see a mountain. Oh, the times I heard, "Hey, there's a mountain out there."

3. One can't really put into words visiting Washington, DC, where I was going to become a general. But that's another story. The ambience, buildings, and art, among other things, overwhelms one. Looking at President Lincoln sitting in his memorial chair, hands on both arms of his chair: the left one open, the right curled up. I could not move from my spot. I stood there a long time imagining it all. To actually see his stovepipe hat in the Smithsonian stunned me. The residence across from the Ford Theatre, where Lincoln was taken after he was shot, was sadly, closed. A man opened the door and I asked when it might open. "Don't move." Fifteen minutes later it opened. In that small bedroom it was hard to imagine his 6'4" frame in that tiny, short bed.

4. A friend and I had scheduled a trip to NYC to tour (again), and see some Broadway shows. We were to arrive the second week of October 2001. After the Twin Towers, we were not sure what to do, but decided to stay with our plans. After checking in, we went to ground zero. The first thing was a smell I could not try to explain. A few people were walking down a driveway and we followed. I looked around. Where were we? Ground Zero. I literally couldn't move. Full trucks with coverings drove past us and out of the hole. A policeman came up and said we were not supposed to be there. We all apologized and left. Many, many years before, I had been at the top of one of the towers.

5. Love to tell you a lot about Key West, but I was in college and don't remember all of it. Well, maybe the nude beach. Got a great tan.

Out of the blue, some twenty-odd years ago, Linda called me. She and a travelling companion decided it was time not to travel further. She called and asked me if I would like to go to London. I told her my name was Tweed, and not Rockefeller, and could not afford the exorbitant price of $600. And that included air fare and hotel. Outrageous, I know. So, off we went to London. I loved being somewhere and having a guide tell us what happened at a certain place. When asked why I didn't buy a book before I went, I always replied, "If I buy a book, why go? " Anne Boylen was beheaded by a single stroke on the north side of the White Tower. As a group of us stood there, hearing this information, Linda was looking up. I asked her why. "Just think, Buddy, she could have been executed on a day not unlike today." Suddenly, 15 people looked up.

7. It's true. Learn some words/sayings in the language where you are going. It can start with hello and good-bye, and add as you learn. They really light up knowing you are trying. And I must confess, it makes me feel so bilingual. *S'il vous plait.* (Of course, I had to look it up).

8. Told to get to the Louve early, by golly, and we were there and 50th in line (or so). Ninety percent of the people started running to see the Mona Lisa. When we heard that, we ran, too. Confusing for me, because I have seen umpteen million copies. Now, I am looking at the real one. A man whispered to his wife, "What if the original is out being cleaned and this is a replica?" Group laugh.

The best part of travelling is coming home.

Thank you for travelling with TT/Tweed Tours.

I want a dime for every time some local, national, or international person begins their story with the word, "Well."

Let's go to the movies. And these snippets are only a few of movie "Ooops" I love. I am sure there are umpteen billion sights for this, like the infamous Starbucks coffee cup on the set of "Game of Thrones" that went undetected. And, you probably have your own special Ooops. Mine are:

    1. In three frames of "The Wizard of Oz," Dorothy's braids go from her shoulders to her chest when she sits and talks to the Scarecrow. 1. Dorothy talks. Braids at shoulders. 2. Scarecrow talks. 3. Dorothy, apparently so enthralled with the Scarecrow, grows her braids to her chest in the third frame. And for eons I never noticed, so caught up was I with the movie.

    2. Up there in top two: "Foul Play," with Goldie Hawn and Chevy Chase, had a murderer breaking into her apartment. He throws her so she is sitting on the bed, him (from his angle) holding her wrists so they are on her chest. From Goldie's point of view (POV in movie chat), her arms are out thrust so as to be seen by the camera. Sooo, as they go back and forth, Goldie looks like a cheerleader, arms opening and closing.

    3. Top one: Morton DaCosta is the famous theatre and film director who helmed such classics 1950's hit Broadway productions of "Plain and Fancy," "No Time for Sergeants," "Auntie Mame," and "The Music Man." He produced and directed the films "Auntie Mame," "The Music Man," and "Island of Love." The reason for this stellar introduction is because I attended a workshop where he was the teacher. We were to direct short scenes, and he would critique. Tec (Teek),

as he was called, was this white-haired, short, chubby man we all instantly fell in love with. Sometimes, to our delight, he would stray away and start telling stories, which we preferred over the critiques he gave. Some of his gems:

1. He was in the original cast of "The Skin of our Teeth," starring Tallulah Bankhead. She had had relationships with both men and women. Tec caught her eye, and she propositioned him. He politely declined, telling her he was gay. Not missing a beat, she told him she would convert him. Never happened.

2. He was asked to direct the movie musical, "Mame," but he had directed the stage play and movie of "Auntie Mame," so he passed.

3. BIG FINISH. And I DO mean BIG. A scene was being filmed in the movie where Rosalind Russell (Mame), and Forrest Tucker (Beauregard Burnside), were in a long shot, with the two walking toward the camera. Mame starts to walk ahead to talk to her nephew, Patrick. Cut. Print. Tec ordered the leaves to be taken off the trees (they were bare before) and take everything down. Some of the crew came up and frantically asked him to stop. He brushed them off. This is important. Well, it can wait until I have this down. No. No, you have to listen now. Tec finished the tear down and then turned to the few crew members. What? Nothing now, one stated. We were trying to tell you that in the long shot that Forrest's dick was swinging back and forth in his pants, as he wore no underwear!! AND, it was not small. Of course, we sat transfixed and laughing. Tec took us to a side room and produced a VHS of the movie, pre-set to that scene. Yes, we had to/wanted to, watch it twice. Enjoy the BIG long shot. Sidebar: When the weekend was over, I asked a friend, (who was on the staff), if she thought he would mind

taking a picture with me. She sm
that after he saw my blocking, n
good."

He also autographed his picture from the
book. Great stories from the great Morton DaCo

* * * * * * * * * * * * * * * * * *

On more than one occasion we have noted my skills in
the math department. So, when I got a new cell phone I
asked for an easy number. He said how about (making
this up) 555-6742) I said that was not easy enough. A
pause. Well, he did have a number he was going to turn
back in because no one would take it. 555-*666. No
hesitation as I took the number. Leaving, I told him if I
dropped dead before I left the store, the 666 was a
curse. Here I sit typing, so I guess we can debunk that
theory. And, easy to remember. Sometimes when I have
to give it out the person will either move on or make a
mention of the last three numbers.

I want you to know how your American dollars went to
good use in Viet Nam, for me and the other rascals. For
example, we went on patrol, following buses because
people who were riders were being shot/shot at as they
rode. Now let us analyze this. American troops were
following a bus so passengers would not be shot.
Meanwhile, we in the jeep were totally exposed, begging
the question: Why shoot in the bus when the soldiers in
the open jeep are sitting ducks? At the end of my first
ride, we took off our goggles and looked at each other
and guffawed. We all looked like racoons because of the
black exhaust farting in our faces as we followed.

Jake Ryan. "Sixteen Candles." Where are your parents?
How did you get the house so clean after the barbells
fell through two floors/expensive wine bottles were

1. At a wh... iess was slow. The head Madam told many of the girls they could go home for a few days. Suddenly, a men's convention came to town, unexpectedly. One of the girls came to the Madam and asked what they were going to do? The wise Madam came up with an idea. "Since the men will be so drunk they won't remember anything, get out our blow-up dolls we use at parties." As the evening went on, all of the real girls were busy. The next customer was taken to a room that had a blow-up doll. It was only a few minutes before he returned and slurred: "I have a complaint and want my money back." "Why?" he was asked. "I bit her on the tit, she farted, and blew out the window."

2. Three elderly women sat in rocking chairs at the home. The first one reminisced, "My husband had six car dealerships and we had a wonderful life." The second chimed in, "My husband owned ten oil wells, and we travelled the world." The third said, "My husband was not rich, but we had a wonderful life. I will say that when he was happy, six birds could stand on it." First: "Well, I think we should tell the truth. My husband only had two dealerships." Second: "If we're going to tell the truth, we only had three oil wells." Third: 'If you're going

to tell the truth, so will I. That sixth bird had to stand on one leg."

TMI: You may not want to read this snippet. That was dumb! Writing that would make you want to read it. Proceed with caution!

I had to do my business, standing. I pulled down my sweatpants and about passed out. On my privates were red bumps. Red bumps. Your life flashes before you (WOW!), and you imagine you only have 2 minutes to live. I reached down to pick off a red spot if I could. I did, and brought it up for inspection. What I was holding was red lint from the new red sweatpants I had put on.

Vienna: Linda and I sitting by a window having breakfast. Two workers with their vests walk by. Linda smiled. "One of those workers had on a T-shirt that said 'Sooners.'" (University of Oklahoma). I ran to our room to get my camera and ran out to find him. I tried English, but he did not understand. I asked his partner if he did, and he said a little. I explained the word on his T-shirt. He laughed and relayed the message. Picture: My right arm on his shoulder, and the left pointing to the word 'Sooner'. He is smiling. Small world and all that jazz.

Oh, for Pete's sake, you would think, by the way I live, I was brought up during the depression.

1. To get all the toothpaste out, I use my toothbrush to keep pushing up the goo until I have turned it every way but loose.

2. The curtain in my bedroom is red satin with red tassels on one side. That is the same curtain made when we did the musical, "Gypsy", which we did in the

mid-80s. Still works. Okay, maybe a few worn spots, but not enough to buy a new one. Skinflint.

3 In high school, on a trip driving to Kansas City, we stopped at a restaurant. For dessert, I ordered a cheesecake. When it came to me, it looked like a tiny, miniscule, had-to-look-twice-to-see-it, slice of cheesecake. I noted that to my mom and dad, more than once. How could they charge the outrageous price of one dollar for dessert? Mother asked me if I was paying for it. I said no, and she said, "Then, shut up."

A substitute teacher at the high school was named Annie Body. She got a lot of work because when a teacher was asked if they had someone in mind, they would answer, "Get Anybody." (Rim shot/true story.)

People can expect so much from me. Take the time teachers went on strike and walked around the Capitol holding up signs. Some friends I was with told me (the drama teacher) I needed to do something the next day to bring attention to our plight. The next day Chuckles shows up dressed as the Grim Reaper, holding a big sign that read: Teachers. A dying breed?

Several photographers jumped in front of me with lots of clicks of the camera. Shortly thereafter, I saw my picture in USA Today. Not only that, but some Jewel Box patrons told me they were in Europe, and one of their friends commented on a picture of someone in Oklahoma. She gasped, knowing it was me.

Sometimes, booking a flight can get one rattled. I tried to book a flight to Charleston, SC, for a former student's wedding. The woman told me I would leave OKC at 9 a.m., and arrive in Denver at ... Hold the phone, I'm going to Denver to get to Charleston? I'll look around.

Toilet paper: Over or under? It is so obvious it's over so you don't have to bend over to find the end, especially if it's stuck on the roll, which means you might accidently ... Over, for sure.

Let's talk clothes. I was never a clotheshorse for labels, etc. I bought what I liked. For some reason, while teaching, the guys would ask me: How many Tommy Hilfiger shirts do I own? How would I know, I don't count? Got home: I had 12. The guys used to love to tease me because I wore my Army issued jacket in the winter. Endless teasing. Imagine their surprise one day when they walked in, ready to pounce, and saw a raccoon coat draped on my chair. They all ran to it, gasping, snorting, touching it. OMG, they gasped: Neiman Marcus. End of taunting. I paid it out because it was a whopping $400. (Still wear it when really cold).

Before I got an actual teaching job, I substituted. A lot, because the lady who called for substitutes liked me. I was more than thrilled when I got a two month stint in El Reno, OK, 27 miles from home. I had a roommate who wore the same size as myself: Shirt, pants, shoes. It was toward the end of the first month, and I got asked how many clothes did I have, because I had not worn the same thing twice. Had to think, but I hadn't, and did not wear the same anything the entire time. Observant, huh?

Teaching. Students are spellbound. Ok, just listening. One student raised his hand. Yes? Mr. Tweed, your shoes don't match. I looked down. I had put on two different shoes dressing in the dark so as not to disturb my sleeping wife. Went home after class. Oh, those little buggers.

Scary costume. At Lyric, in the musical "Sugar," Don and I put on our costumes for the big number 'When You

Meet a Man in Chicago' toward the end of the show. We were in a leotard, like women wear that have the sides cut up, like the one Pam Anderson wore on 'Baywatch.' We tried to hide our package and all types of tricks. We went to what is called a costume parade, where the entire cast comes out in one row and the director and costumer have you step forward and comment on the costume.

When they came to me, I had put on a tiny skirt I had found. The director asked me what I was doing. I told him I did not want the audience to wonder where my goods were during the number. I was told to step back in line. When we were excused, many of the cast said it was so nice working with me, but they felt I was about to be fired. Went to lunch and came back to altered costumes.

I offer you a gift: a blank slate. As your day begins, take the 'slate' and write down things. It can be anything. Things you want to accomplish. Not necessarily big things. Maybe give someone a compliment/say thank you (a lot)/offer help if you can/don't let someone ruin your day with their negativity. Add to your own list. At the end of the day, how did you do? Best part? The next day you wipe it clean and start anew. For me, the beauty is that each day is new. Sure, some things did not get solved, or you did not accomplish something, but hey, you get that blank slate the next day. Good luck and you're welcome.

Oh, how the internet just buzzes over things. One I enjoy is, "What's next?" For example, I binge-watched a show. After the last episode the internet was all abuzz with people asking what happened to the characters after the ending? One site even talked to actors in the show I watched, asking them what they thought their characters did after the finale. Really? What happened to my fake character after the ending???

* * * * * * * * * * * * * * * * * *

While at Ft. Lewis, I found where a new movie version of "Peter Pan" was going to be made, but with a twist. If the audience did not clap to bring Tinkerbell back to life, the projectionist would skip to a second reel where Peter looks at the audience and says something like: "You did not clap and now Tink is dead! You killed her!"

I am sure that no kids would be traumatized and turn out to be serial killers later in life for that peachy surprise. Can you imagine picking up your crying, hysterical child, screaming they just killed Tinkerbell. And, as an adult, the person wakes up in the middle of the night screaming, "I killed Tinkerbell." To answer the obvious question: No, it did not get made.

For years and years my mother would say when she went, it would be in the fall, when it was pretty and cool. Change of plans. She went in the sweltering heat of July, and in the middle of rehearsals of a play I was in. Not a good theatrical ending for sure. At least it was not as long a time as my sister.

Don't think badly of me, but my brother-in-law told me of a conversation he had with my sister, after two years of her declining health. She was toward the end (but lingered), and he said she suddenly blurted out, "I see the light. I see the light." I told him, like in the movie "Poltergeist," "Tell her to go to the light!" Pause, and we both laughed.

Batteries. Aren't they something else? You put them in some device, point, and it works. Until the battery goes kaput. What died in the battery? Like a microwave. You watch and whatever is in there begins to cook/bubble/burn. Yet, you don't see anything like a flame, electric burner, a match.

* * * * * * * * * * * * * * * * * *

Wanna play hopscotch? We can hop around with some fun thoughts:

1. Which three words would you like to be remembered for, as I asked earlier? Duh, like someone would actually include egotistical, rude, liar, thief, gossip, etc., which might make the list if you were truthfully answering.

2. What would you tell your younger self? First of all, my younger self is not around, and it might be a little late to tell him anything about what his life will have in store.

3. Who would you invite to your fantasy dinner party? I love this one. Picture it: you invite people who, perhaps, have nothing in common. So, they have to be introduced to one another, and God forbid they don't like one another and get in a huge fight even before the salad plate hits the table.

4. Name someone in your profession from the past you wish you could have worked with? You can't, they're dead.

5. How would you answer a reporter who, after a traumatic event, asks you: What was going through your mind at that time? Maybe something like: "Well, I do have to get some milk and eggs on the way home." I know, I know, the public loves those types of questions.

6. What kind of tree/animal/flower best describes you? No comment.

7. I think people who drive into water and get stuck and have to be pulled out should have to pay, at the very least, a hefty fine. Same for the person who says, after having their vehicle taken (sometimes with children inside), "We were only in there two seconds." Two seconds? Really?

My feet hurt from hopping. Moving on....

* * * * * * * * * * * * * * * * * * * *

I admit there is a lot I don't know or understand.

The debt ceiling is in the news now. What is a debt ceiling? Where does the money come from and go? Trillions? Is that like an American Express card?

Does your zodiac sign really describe you? Who thought them up and picked the dates for that sign? Why am I asking you?

I think I can save money. I buy dressings and sauces and pour them on some things I eat. I can't really taste the product all covered in goo. Buying a container of Ranch dressing or steak sauce will allow me to just suck some out of the bottle.

Whether you believe in ghosts, or whatever, is up to you. But I can't argue with someone who says this or that happened or what they saw. I'm not necessarily into a UFO story, but...I was awakened in bed one night when I felt like something was gently pulling on my toes over the covers. After 3 seconds it stopped.

Another time I had my back to the edge of the bed, and I awoke to feel like someone was gently rubbing on my back. Again, stopped after a few seconds. It was not like I was drowsy from being awakened because I was fully awake. What was not any of the above was someone who lived in the apartment below me who had moved out.

We talked a few times, and he was a very nice middle-aged man. When I asked the office about his moving, they told me he gave several reasons. First, the black woman who would take my trash out, put it on the back of my car, and drive it to the dumpster would ignore him. She never existed. Second, the two kids I had in my apartment made too much noise. No kids. And the kicker ... he swore I had a woman in a coffin in my closet. I do believe in spooks, I do believe in spooks.

Take your seats and get out your notebooks, and let's begin our class on driving. At one time or another this has to have happened to you.

Driving. It is clearly marked that the three lanes will become two with big arrows on the pavement indicating it is time to merge. So, I tootle along. On the far left some cars go by at a high rate of speed until there is nowhere to go. They had gone by at least ten or more cars to get to that spot. And, sure enough, nice people let them cut in.

Au contraire! I waited in line and so can you. When not let in, they begin to slither into the lane. Sometimes it works, sometimes it does not. And sometimes, I get a thumbs up from the driver. Wait a minute, that wasn't a thumb, after all.

To blink or not to blink. At times a car will move in front of me with no blinker and I have to tap my brakes, or you can see other drivers' taillights turn red ahead as they are also cut off. Or driving, when someone has had their blinker on for 30 seconds, and you're not sure whether to slow down, move over or honk your horn.

It is well established I don't do car anything's, but this just popped in my head. My dashboard indicated my right rear tire was low. I dutifully put air in it. It would not show it was full. I put in more and then drove off. I Googled places where they check tire pressure and lo and behold, I saw one as I came out of the bank drive-through. He bent down and put on the tire pressure thingamabob.

He did it twice and stood up. I explained what I saw on the dashboard and what I had done. "Uh, Sir, it has too much air. Like 96 pounds, when the normal pressure for your car is 36. I did not know it would hold that much." He reduced the amount, and I profusely thanked him and asked him not to tell the story until I had driven off.

Two items that we get furious at when they stop, but work non-stop for us all other times: cars and phones. We use them all the time. But, let them mess up one time, and one would think the world was about to end.

Don't know why, when or how, but for some reason I had to have a Hard Rock something every time I went there. I collected a lot from all over here and abroad. BUT, I have to buy it, it can't be given to me. I did not mean to hurt a student's feelings, but he brought me a T-shirt from Egypt his father brought back for me. Crazy, I know, and realized I should have taken it and given it as a gift to someone. Ungrateful bastard!! If you want to borrow a baseball cap from me from HR, you have your pick (to name a few) Rome, New York, Acapulco, Athens, Heidelberg, Hollywood, Moscow, and Honolulu. Don't get me started on the T's.

I have always dreamed of directing something on Broadway. From all my travels, New York City still electrifies me. It's energy always makes me happy. I never get tired of it.

The first thing I do when I come home is take off my watch and ring.

I always change to something comfortable and wear only socks around ye olde apartment.

While travelling I saw this sign: Emergency Exit. Press bar for 3 seconds. Door will open in 15 seconds. Uh, say what??

JC Penney: I want my money back. Until 2022 I had one of your microwaves. The timer on it had been out a long time, and I had to buy an egg timer. The microwave weighed a ton! The size of a small safe. Serial No: MY00711. Manufactured: September 1977. Yes, I had to add 3 minutes to each use, but I just could not get rid of it. We had been through a lot. When I had someone help me put it in the dumpster, he took a picture of it, too.

I have never lost a key.

Just to jazz someone's day I would call an office for an appointment or whatever, and speak with a foreign accent and say, "I would like to order a pizza." They would tell me I had the wrong number. I would repeat my order. Same response from them. Loved hearing them laugh. I had to stop on some when I tried to order and they responded, "Hi, Chuck."

When shootings started taking place years ago and I was teaching a movie making class, I would hear/see a person on TV say the student(s) made graphic movies of killing. Three fourths of my students did the same thing, but it was a different time. The principal called me to his office where I met a student's mother. She told me he was becoming strange because he was looking at books on witchcraft for the movie. I talked to him afterwards, and he said she was crazy, and it was for the movie.

After a few chats she let him stay with his group, and after the movie, he went back to "normal."

I saw on a sun dial: "Time Erases all but Memories"

We can all relate to the movie "It's a Wonderful Life." Think of all the people you have known, loved, touched, encouraged and how they, in turn, made your life wonderful. Ironically, as I write, it is Teacher Appreciation Week, and boy, do I thank mine. I know there was a teacher you admired. And some of my student teachers who were going to become exceptional in their craft.

One female student teacher, who will go unnamed, was teaching and I was in the back of the room. Sometimes to get their attention, I would whack my paddle on the podium. That day, the vice-principal decided to observe. We both sat at the back, him with his legal pad and pen.

He looked down to write something, which is the exact time she decided to whack said paddle on said podium. I looked over and his pen was ripping up the legal pad from bottom to top as he yelped. Chaos for about 15 seconds to calm everyone down. Did not give her a good recommendation, but saw her the next year at a speech contest. Aghast, I asked her what she was doing. A small school district had hired her.

In junior high I had a math teacher who was a little robust. Shirt, tie, pants. We used to giggle amongst ourselves, wondering what he wore in the summer and could not imagine him in (yuk) shorts. What goes around....One day, teaching, a hand went up. Yes? Mr. Tweed, what do you wear in the summer? Shell shock. Uh, shorts. You wear shorts? Full circle moment for the history books.

* * * * * * * * * * * * * * * * * * *

Some things I would like to do:

Learn to fly an airplane.

Speak at least two languages fluently. Hell, I'd settle for one.

Own stock in Google/Twitter/Facebook/etc.

Grow hair.

Some things I would never do:

Bungee jump.

Jump out of an airplane.

Wash windows on a high-rise anything.

Be a bull fighter.

After my car/Jeep stories, I now think it funny I worked at two car dealerships. Before Lynn Hickey I worked at Gandra Buick, filing, doing titles and working the customer service desk in the lobby. Gay, who was the main receptionist, came back from lunch. I was talking to one of the salesman, Eddie, who was Black. She held out her right hand and exclaimed: "Look," as she started to pull the ring off. "I bought this ring, and I thought it was gold. It's not and now it's turning my finger black."

Eddie's eyes went wide, and he put his hand on the counter, saying "That's how mine started."

When I came in one day, some of the office staff told me Gay had had a window peeper. As a single woman it could be quite scary, I thought. I immediately went to the desk. She said she saw him at the window and ran out, chasing him and screaming. Incredulous, I asked if she was cussing him out, and not missing a beat, she smiled, "Hell no, I was going to ask him to come back".

Working there I told the salesmen to look out for a used car for me. I did not want one with an air conditioner that did not come with the car. I was told they found a great car. A light blue car (my favorite color) and when I got in and saw the air conditioner installed under the dash, I balked. Salesman told me we were going to take a test drive. It was a hot summer day. We left, he turned on the A/C, and by time we got back to the dealership my nuts were knocking. I bought it. Loved that car. Got several complaints about turning it down because it felt like ten degrees.

I graduated mid-term, so I signed up to substitute with the Oklahoma City Public School. Luckily, the woman who called prospective substitutes liked me, and I got called practically every day. Sometimes, being so exhausted from the day before (yeah, right!), I did not answer. When I first started, I knew I would not take anything from the students. They would know who was boss. I would be sure to monitor when they took a breath, blink, or sneezed.

I was usually at one of my schools for about a week. On the third day at one junior high, this one student was lingering. Uh, oh, here it comes, a student who was going to start something. He walked up, looked me in the eyes, and said, "Mr. Tweed, we like you, we really do. But you don't have to be so hard on us. We're good kids." And he walked out. I sat down in shock. He was absolutely correct. Needless to say, the kinder Mr. Tweed sprang forth and we had a great time. Out of the mouths of babes.

At this one high school I was told there was a student teacher who was lecturing on "Julius Caesar," and I would take over when she was finished. I sat in the back corner. She, dressed in her sarape and jeans, was explaining Roman times and that there were lots of orgies back then.

My eyes went to hub cap size as she explained what an orgy was. Not too graphic, but they got the idea. As she finished, she told them: "Now, don't do to Mr. Tweed what you did to the last substitute, when you stood up with your desk and banged them on the floor." The class turned to me, and my eyes went to slits. They looked at each other, no doubt thinking they had better not try that.

I was lucky enough to get a nine week assignment in El Reno, about thirty minutes from the city. I had so much fun. Years later I was talking to a vice-president at the Daily Oklahoman about something with the Jewel Box, and she asked me a question. She wanted to know if I taught at El Reno, because she played Peppermint Patty in a production of "Charlie Brown." I said yes. The famous musical had not come out, so I strung together several snippets (great choice of words, huh?) and we put on a show. The cafeteria was packed. At the end they were instructed to take their curtain call and exit.

They bowed but just stood there, I tried to wave them off from the back. Two students did leave. I got on a chair and attempted to direct them to leave. A cast member called my name. The audience turned, applauding, to see me standing on a chair waving them off. I froze. They brought out a huge, and I do mean *huge*, Snoopy as a gift. I walked up and we all hugged. I kept that dog until he could no longer stand.

* * * * * * * * * * * * * * * * * *

I'm going to throw this out. It reflects a time long, long ago, so keep any negative opinions to yourselves. Thank you. It was the late 60s and, at that time, this school had students stand for the Pledge of Allegiance. On cue, with the intercom telling the students to stand, one male sat there with crossed arms. I asked him to please stand. He did not. Lowering my voice, I told him I respected his not wanting to pledge, but he would stand for the flag itself. He stood.

My go-to Karaoke song is...wait a minute, I don't do Karaoke.

I must pay homage to my typing teacher in high school. She gave me such a gift that kept me in offices typing for captains and majors because I was so good. Note to those still learning. Do NOT look at the keys when you type. You will learn to type faster and more accurately. If you currently use the hunt-and-peck method, that's okay too, because there are some really fast finger poppers out there.

So, we were taking a typing test before basic, and I finished and sat there. The male to my left did the same. Nothing to do, so we took our page to the front desk. He panicked and told us to go finish, and we said we had. Bingo! My future was set.

Captain MacKey was head of the Overseas Replacement Station at Ft. Lewis, where soldiers waited to be shipped out (and where I was sent out). He was a stickler about no mistakes or erasures. As head clerk I did all the typing for him. I got to the bottom—the bottom—of the page and made a boo-boo. I just knew he would allow one minor correction at the bottom. NOT! Out he came and put it on my desk.

When a Lt. called, asking for him, and I did not know where he was, off he went on me. I don't remember what I said defending myself, but the Cpt. called me in and told me the Lt. said I was rude. Cpt. said in the future he would always tell me where he was going, but I might need to watch my tone. Duly noted. I liked him. The Cpt., not the &^%#@ Lt.

So many fun memories while there. Gordon (last names only) lived in Silverton, WA, and he told us that the three of us comrades (Gordon made four) should come to his property and cut our own Christmas trees. Wow wow and wow!! Off we went in Ron's Volkswagen (don't ask) to cut our booty. I can still see all those gorgeous trees standing there. We each picked the perfect tree and tied three trees on the top of the car. Well, kinda.

They covered the entire car, so it looked like trees rolling down the highway on their own. The next day someone told us to watch the news. At a local station they had captured us putt-putting down the highway, the only thing visible to indicate it was a car was where we had to part said trees so Ron could see out of the windshield. Got home. My eyes must have thought my apartment was three stories high, and I had to cut off at least four feet from the bottom. Gorgeous tree!

Went to Seattle a few times with two buds who liked theatre. We just had to go when we heard Margaret Hamilton (yes, that one) was in a play. When she came out, we would not stop applauding until she put her hands up for us to stop. I know many of you have seen an important person and remember it like it was yesterday.

I was in a one act play at a community theatre just off base. To save time, they allowed me to do my white make-up at home and get in my white costume. I sprayed my hair (which I had then) white, and drove to the theatre. I had to change my course somewhat when some man, driving through an intersection, saw me and gently bumped the back of the car in front of him. From that point on, if I stopped, turned right and then turned around in a parking lot to go left, I was fine.

Except, the one time I cut it close. My cat was having kittens and Daddy Chuck had to be there. I had to. She was a very expensive cat, costing 99 cents outside some store with cats and dogs for sale. Cute black and white kitten. We were inseparable. She would lay on my legs as we watched TV and when I slept on my stomach, she slept between my legs curled up. I never remember having rolled over on her. She was a quick learner. One time while I was shaving and she was sitting on the closed toilet lid, she jumped on my leg while I was in my underwear. Without thinking, I batted at her gently. Stopped that one. She was casually sitting on the edge of the tub while I took a bath. I knew it was bound to happen as she gently walked the rim, trying to be with me. In she went and out she went!

Shipped her home with me and stayed together until she was ten.

Under me in the apartment was what used to be a café. In it were like 8-10 sets of ice cream tables and chairs. I wanted one. Badly. When I was moving out, I bought one for $50. That was like 1967. And guess what? It's still in mint condition. In fact, I have used it so many times in shows I did at the Jewel Box, one patron, standing at the top of the stairs before entering, smiled, saying, "Must be your show."

"How do you know?"

"Isn't that your table and chairs?"

Okay, I'll take 40% blame on this one me, the other 60...well, you will soon see. Because I had two jobs, I never watched late night TV, so when a friend and I went to New York, and she wanted to get tickets to her favorite late-night host, I said okay. We stood with a group as we moved into the lobby to get tickets. A man talked to us on how important it was to be a good audience. *Really?* I thought. So, he keeps yapping and we get our tickets. Then we go on the other side of the split lobby to exit where we were stopped by yet another man telling us the host would do a dry run. That is to come out and see what kind of audience members we would be. The more we reacted, the better the show.

I was getting a little prickly about that time, but said nothing. So, later that afternoon we are standing in line awaiting entry. We were like 8-9 in line. I stepped up and a man asked me for my ID. This is the 40% part. I said I did not carry one, but was told I needed to produce one. I asked why they did not mention that tiny item when we got our tickets, and he said something I don't remember.

I ran, and I do mean ran, back to the hotel. You know a New York City block is long. I did not stop running until I got back. When we finally got in, we were in the second to last row in the balcony, when we surely would have been front and center had we been let in as we were in line. When the guest came in, I could not see him because a TV monitor was hanging in the balcony blocking where he was sitting, and I had to lean to the right or left to see. So glad I did not set off a smoke alarm, as my ears began to sizzle. PS: He was not someone I wanted to see, anyway. If you disagree, well tuff. T-U-F-F. When you write your own snippets you can comment.

Sometimes, upon seeing a New York show, I was among those standing for an autograph after the show. "My One and Only" with Tommy Tune and Twiggy was delightful, so I just had to buy a poster and Sharpie for them to sign afterwards. I can only imagine what I must have looked like when they came out.

They scanned the group, and Twiggy and I locked eyes. She immediately came to me and signed my poster, followed by Tommy. I thought how pathetic I must have looked for her to walk to me. A lost soul with a poster standing there with a Sharpie. Who cares? I got the autographs, which over time, have faded from the framed poster I still have.

Was going to skip remarking on this show, but here goes. The friend I was with had bought tickets to a show as a surprise. I thought of which great Broadway show it might be. Probably she had ordered the tickets months in advance because they were sold out long in advance. I was really hyped all day. Off we go. I turn the corner, and on the marquee in giant letters reads: "Puppetry of the Penis."

Let's give credit where it is due. Man, those two guys could do some spectacular tricks with their penises. Don't know what the other men were thinking, but mine hurt a little bit as we left the theatre thinking of trying even one of those twisters. Right now, wiggling in my chair as I write. Calm down, down there, I'm not going to do any puppetry.

* * * * * * * * * * * * * * * * * * *

Like everyone, I sometimes dream of winning the lottery, but one has to buy a ticket first, which I have never done.

For a while I had a passion for watches. Well, fake ones I bought in the Village. I told everyone they were fake, but they sure looked good. When my 'Rolex' battery stopped I went to get a new one. He looked at it and said they could not replace it as it was fake. I saved it for years hoping it might all change and I could wear my 'Rolex.' Today, I might get mugged over it, and the thieves would come back and kill me when they found out it was fake.

One of my favorite songs in college was "Scotch and Soda." Still is. So, I thought I'd try one. Also, thought I might sue the bar for giving me battery acid. Yuck. More power to those who love it.

I twitch like there is no tomorrow if I am around people, and they start cracking their knuckles.

Here we go with another smoking jaunt.

As noted, Sis smoked. When she went to college she joined a sorority, where they taught her to smoke. When she came home and pulled out a pack of cigs, I was in shock. Sis...smoking? "How cool is that?" thought the senior in high school. We were always good friends, and when I told her one morning I wished I had $5 for something, she gave it to me.

When she went back to OSU, I, too, wanted to be cool like my sister and bought a pack of cigarettes. Mother came in that night and saw them on my desk and asked what was up and I told her I was going to try smoking. She said okay and left the room. Here goes. Buddy is going to light up and be cool. My mother came back in the room after she heard me coughing up a lung.

Moving on to when I was in a show at the Jewel Box where the script said I smoked, which you could back then. I lit it and wham, bam, thank you ma'am. It took me back to the night at my desk turning green. The director, once I was able to breathe again, said we would cut it. I have never been able to inhale.

During a show, an actor was smoking in a scene we had where he sat in a chair, and I was on the couch. We were to both stand up at the same time. We did. Only he got too close, and his cigarette planted itself right between my eyebrows. His eyes popped, and his hands started slapping at my burn—like a dog does when it wants treats.

We had a few more lines of dialogue and I put my finger in my mouth to get it wet and slowly brought it up to the burnt flesh. Not sure, but there might have been a slight sizzle. I was to run out the door. At that time the doors to the backstage had a peephole. As I ran to the door, I collided with it and slowly went to my knees as the audience went into gales of laughter.

I pushed open the door to find a crew member leaning against the wall. Later, he said he just wanted to watch the show and had just peeked into the peep hole. And that was even before intermission. Of course, everyone came running to the dressing room where I told the director, I quit!!!! It didn't leave me permanently scarred. In fact, there was no evidence after a day or two that it had even happened.

* * * * * * * * * * * * * * * * * *

I'm one of the lucky people who can put something together and still have parts left over, but it still works.

No one has ever called me Duncan Hines. I called my mother to help me make something and every time she said an ingredient, I told her I did not have it and would substitute with something else. Tasted it, and spit it out. To wisely get rid of it, I put some in the dog's dish, who smelled it, looked at me for at least ten seconds, and promptly walked away.

Men: Raise your hand if you actually open the pocket to pee.

As mentioned before, with my movie making class, I was a frustrated movie director, although I could never do an actual one. As mentioned before...the best laid plans...

At Del City High School, a movie was being made using a rifle. I'll say it anyway: we used blanks. The rule was I had to be there for that portion of any movie with guns/knives/etc. I always notified the office when such a scene was going to be shot, because the office would get a frantic call that there was a sniper on the roof, only to be told it was a movie class.

Picture it: back parking lot at Carl Albert High School full of cars. As fate would have it, the junior high down the street was having graduation, as it were, the day we were filming. For the scene a car would zoom into the parking lot, circle around, and "shoot" someone, who would then fly against the wall and slide down. The car rolls in, only the spotters, yet again, not doing their duty, did not notice the parents and teen-age son walking right into the center of the parking lot. Shots ring out and the family bites the dust as the security guard at the school, who was around 105, comes running, well, shuffling, into the scene, screaming for everybody to get down. Back to square one and re-do the shot with spotters doing their job.

As stated, I was a pretty good shot. At the shooting range in basic, a group of us were vying for best shot. We started at the base line and were to move forward, taking another shot at specified spots. My rifle jammed. Never had that happen. Suddenly, the Lt. of our unit appeared out of nowhere, undid the jam, and as I kept shooting, moved with me, inserting rounds after each shot. He helped me win.

OMG, did we all groan when SSgt Smith told us we would love our weapons like they were our own. Being with the rifle day after day, we learned how to dismantle it and put it back together. At the end of basic we all wanted to take our rifles with us. They did become like a lover you wanted to take care of.

All of us had mama-sons in Vietnam to do our uniforms. They would squat with a towel on the floor and iron. One day mine was unusually quiet. I found out her son had been killed. We did not speak until she started to walk out, and I went with her, trying to say something, anything, to let her know I cared. Don't care how or what one says, it never seems quite right. When I finally got my orders and was going to leave, she asked me if she could come with me and told me how hard she would work for me. Of course, I had to decline.

Went to get groceries yesterday, and when I pulled out some bills, I was reminded about folding bills so you can see the Twin Towers fall.

Will need one each: one/five/ten/twenty, and work from lowest to highest. (Use a one that does not have the word ONE in big letters.).

Hold portrait facing away.

Fold in half and flip so "In God We Trust" faces out.

Crease center and re-open.

Holding at center, turn down the right or left side.

Do the same with the other side.

Turn the bill around. Both should be touching.

In the center are the Twin Towers with the first hits.

The first time I finished, I was amazed. To actually get the bills, fold them just right, and you have a story to tell. Makes me wonder who thought to do the above in the same order.

* * * * * * * * * * * * * * * * *

Coming back from a trip, Linda and I were in line to enter the USA. Came up, handed over passport (I never ever took my driver's license abroad).

The Customs Officer asked for it. WTF? I told him I did not have it and had never carried it. He told us to report to some office. Fuming, we went, AND we were on a limited time to board plane to Oklahoma. Went. Woman at desk, very bored, heard our story and said go sit down. We did, and luckily, got in quickly.

After telling him I never carried my DL and we had a plane to catch, he said okay, looked in his computer, and off we ran! As I walked by the bored lady's desk, I banged on it as I passed just to make her jump. Got close to gate and heard this was last call. Saw a woman in a tram and asked for a ride. We were the last two on the plane in the last two seats. Only time in 19 years was I asked for DL.

Finding the gnomes from "The Sound of Music" in Austria was not easy. We walked and walked and looked and looked. Not finding them we saw a short, cute, little robust woman, dressed in traditional garb offering SOM bicycle rides, and asked her. She said (lower your voice for this one with your best Austrian accent), "In da' garden." Off we went. Again, no garden. We went back and she raised her right hand and waved it around like she was putting a hex on someone as she pointed to where we had just come from and barked (lower voice even deeper), "In da' garden! In da' garden!"

I scrambled off like a puppy being scolded. Walked along a very tall hedge and there it was. A tiny slit in the foliage. Eureka! Gnomes. All of them and had my picture taken with the one in glasses that the children tap as they go by. I had to go back to thank her, but really wanted a picture. No, she did not smile. Even better!

I don't know what women check, but men check their flies before going out, or at the event after you-know-what. I directed "Funny Girl" at Jewel Box. After a scene, an actor came up looking upset. He asked me why I had not told him. Tell him what?

"My fly was open the whole scene, and I don't wear underwear." A pause. I replied: "I wasn't looking at your crotch, but apparently there was not much to see, or I would have noticed." He stormed off and did not speak to me for an hour.

I think we can all agree that looking at some of our teachers (back then), we noticed how they dressed and acted and surmised what miserable lives they led. Not too much fun in class. Jan, Deanne and I put that old myth to rest. Jan taught across the hall from me. One day one of us got bored and played a trick on the other and we were off and running.

Coming back from the auditorium where one class went every day, I always gave my key to a student to go ahead and unlock the door. He did, but stood there frozen with his mouth open. I walked to the door to find all 30 of my chairs missing. A girl called my name and pointed to the entrance of the bathroom while a boy did the same at their bathroom. All of our desks had been put in both bathrooms.

Turnabout is fair play, we figured. So, when Jan and her herd came up the stairs from the library, they had a little trouble, because her 30 chairs were on the stairs, and we stood at the top watching them try to crawl over the chairs and get them back into the room.

Back in class we had no time for this tomfoolery, but decided we did and plotted further revenge. Three days later we walked into her room while she was lecturing, and students walked down the aisles. Suddenly, 20 cans of Silly String popped out and we let them have it.

We teachers knew how to show our students professionalism.

As we neared the end of pranks, I was wondering what the *coup d' etat* could be. Something really stupendous. As my class was spit balling, a hand went up. He told me he had a medium size boa constrictor. Bingo!!! We all got to pet the boa when he took it out of the cage. Slowly I opened Jan's door and the head of the snake started slithering in. No one noticed until the first yell/scream sounded. If I remember correctly, the shuffling of feet trying to get on their desks and Jan running to the far wall screaming, sounded like the running of the bulls in Pamplona.

Imagine our surprise when the principal called us in to reprimand us for our shenanigans. Turns out a teacher down the hall reported us. That person moved downstairs the following year. May have been a little prompting from us to help the move.

Is it no wonder we could not wait to get to school? In our defense, we were really good teachers and the funny stuff along the way made it so much more fun for everyone. I remember, while I was still teaching English early on, students would ask if this was the class that went to a nursing home.

I know how I am going to spend the money from my best seller in my twilight years. Wait a minute, I'm already in the "Twilight Zone"—I mean twilight years. Here's what I am going to do: With all the devices in my life, like Alexa, Siri, Fire Stick, etc., I'm going to sit in my new very plush recliner that holds drinks, snacks and a charging station for my phone and buy a mini fridge and a very nice porta potty so I never have to move far. Brilliant, huh? Well, that's your opinion.

Being Production Director at the original Jewel Box Theatre many people knew me, but with 2,900 season patrons, I did not know many names. Over the years, while out and about, people would approach me and tell me they were season ticket holders. Not quite the introduction I was expecting when I was on my side in my hospital gown, open in the back, exposed for my colonoscopy, and I heard... "Aren't you Chuck Tweed? My mother used to be in shows at Jewel Box." And under I went for my exam. Later, I could only imagine what her mom thought when she told her, "Mom, guess whose ass I went up today?"

When a new teacher came to Carl Albert, we hit it off. He suggested getting a drink one night, and who am I to say no? Although on a well-traveled street, let us say the bar décor was not up to standards. Loved it! We are sitting at a table and it's pretty crowded and noisy. At the end of the bar was a man who had apparently been there for a few hours and was happy, yelling out things, singing to what was on the jukebox (remember those?).

At times he would lean to one side, and I thought he was going to fall off. When one of his favorite songs came on, he really got animated and quite promptly stood up, feet on either side of the stool legs, leaned to the right, and fell onto the man next to him and splattered to the floor. Which was followed by a car crashing into one of the picture windows in the front. Panic and pandemonium. Everyone up and moving.

When we heard the police sirens coming, we decided to make a run for it. Got in the car, but we could not back up due to the police cars, lights flashing in the night. To make a clean get-a-way I decided to go forward. Apparently, I did not notice the small incline before you got on the road. I pressed the accelerator and down we went, then up we went and catapulted onto the street, weaving as I gained control of the somewhat runaway car. We figured it best to not frequent that establishment again.

Not so lucky on our next outing. Walked into the bar. Small entrance. You could go either right or left. Friend started to the left, and wouldn't you know it, one of my students came out of the right door. She hugged me and asked if I would join her. I said yes but would not have a drink. Friend said he would go into the left side. We went in. She had a table that was right in front of a stage. As my eyes adjusted, I noticed there sure were a lot of females sitting close to the stage.

Lights on the stage came up and out came an inebriated young man. The audience cheered. I asked what was going on, and she informed me it was amateur strip night, and this was her boyfriend. Sliding down in my chair, I tried to slip out, but she grabbed my arm in her excitement. Slowly, to the music, he peeled off his shirt. Mind going crazy.

How much strip was there to amateur strip night?? I looked down. The cheers got louder. I looked up. He was removing his jeans. When the music stopped, off he went in his boxers, and I bolted out the door. My soon to be ex-friend was laughing his ass off. As we were leaving, out came my student and her boyfriend. She introduced him and beamed that out of six contestants he won the $100 prize.

When people try to scare me and I don't jump, I tell them that Ray, in my first hour, scared it all out of me. Apparently, it was his mission in life to scare me anytime, anywhere. He would pop out of the darndest places. I sat at my desk to call roll one day and felt a hand grab my knee, which made said knee fly up and bang on the desk drawer. Hysterical laughter from the room. (Little buggers).

One time a girl told me her locker was jammed. They were rather tiny lockers, and I got the lock open but could not pull the door open. When I did, Ray came flying out and Mr. Tweed went flying across the hall, banged into the lockers and slid down to the floor.

Finally, the perfect opportunity came to get him back. Walking to the office from my room in the main hall was a very long trophy case. In the glass, I saw Ray, coming in late from an appointment, slowly walking down the hall. I pressed myself against the wall that was curved so I was not seen. I could not wait to see his shoes and jump out. I saw the tip of a shoe, and out I jumped with a whoop. The sophomore girl, clutching her books, too scared to scream, started wheezing for breath as she slowly sank to her knees in terror.

I helped her up as I profusely kept apologizing and guided her a few steps toward her room. She went out of sight, and Ray came up. "Did I hear someone wheezing?" he asked. I said no. He said he thought he had, but stopped to use the restroom before coming to class.

Don't you love gifts that keep on giving? My grandfather had a few oil wells, and when my grandmother passed, the shares were passed to mom, then to sis, brother and me. At first, they were a nice sum. Nothing major, but when I started getting my share it was around $300. As the years went by, the amount dropped. There were two wells. On one of them I got a letter stating that because it was not much, they would save up for three months, and then send a check. Had to laugh when I received my $27.00 check, which is now down to $12.00. Yesterday I got a check from the other well for $57.00. Not bad after all these years, huh?

As stated earlier, I try and be a good flyer. Was boarding out of OKC and got pulled. Had no idea why. A man, wife, and two younger kids (around 7-8), were in front of me, and the blithering gate person was going through some things and commenting. He pulled out a magazine. One of those that has a bikini-clad woman on an expensive motorcycle. He held it up, commented on it.

The dad indicated he needed to continue and cut the comments. As the gate person was doing his 'comedy' routine, I noticed two women were at the counter, chatting away. I stepped up, and he looked at my carry-on, not in. He began to frisk me. He decided to comment on something as his hand began to creep up my leg. When it got a little too close to my crotch (I felt,) I said, rather loudly: 'You get any higher and we are going to be engaged.'

People behind me started laughing, he got flustered and told me to move on. He forgot to stamp my ticket to indicate he had done his job. One of the women said I did not have it stamped, and I informed her he was too busy with his routine to stamp it, and I was boarding. She looked at the comedian, who did not look at me, but blubbered to let me board.

I always have my seatbelt on. Landing in Park City, Utah, the plane suddenly dropped so fast that anything not held down was flying, which included two little girls across from me and in the back of one row. Splat in the aisle one went. I tried to reach her, but could not. Besides, we were flying level now. When we landed, and you know how people like to undo their seat belts before the plane stops, I heard two clicks and turned to see the girls undoing their belts as we continued to roll up for departure. I turned and snapped, "Keep you belts fastened," which they did.

When we stood up to exit, I noticed the mother was sitting behind me holding a baby. She smiled and thanked me. The event was in the next morning's paper. As I exited the plane, I realized I had bumped my head pretty hard. Small bump, which allowed me to be overly dramatic for a few hours. Now that I think about it, I only had a small headache.

* * * * * * * * * * * * * * * * * *

If you were cast in one of my shows and female, you could find yourself knocked up. A trait of mine I only discovered after someone told me that certain actresses would become pregnant during the production or shortly thereafter. One even got pregnant *twice* working with her. (Save rude comments) Went to the doctor yesterday and saw two questions: Are you pregnant, and are you breastfeeding? I should have put on my audition form: Do you want to be knocked up during or after the show? Hindsight.

Short one: With the movie making class, at the end of the semester we would watch all of the movies and vote for Best Actor/Actress and Supporting and Best Movie. I went to the trophy place I always frequented. Over the years there have been just a few mistakes, so I decided to look them over. The first one I pulled out was: Best Heifer, Kansas City Livestock Show. The trophies supposedly going to Kansas City were in my hands.

Some heifer in Kansas City was going to be named Best Actor, etc. I know, with the honor, he would have been really moooved. (Rim shot) They let me keep the Best Heifer bowl.

Tom Sheehan and I were cast in a world premiere melodrama at Lincoln Plaza, a dinner theatre in OKC that sat 250 people. The author was directing. There were approximately 15 or so in the cast. I was having a new a/c put in and told the stage manager well in advance I would be there, but might be a few minutes late on the day it was to be put in. I walked in the stage door 15 minutes after rehearsal was to start. I turned the corner, and the entire cast was sitting there in the audience, with the director, who was looking at his watch. I stood center stage.

"Well, Mr. Tweed", he began, "I'm so glad you could make it. You have kept the entire cast waiting to rehearse." I told him I had told the stage manager what was going on at least four days ago. "Well, you know," he reminded me, "You have not signed your contract yet," to which I replied (verbatim), "If you want to punish me, make me stay in this show. To reward me, let me go." Small gasps from the cast. The director walked off. I went and sat down with the cast. A few minutes later the stage manager had me sign my contract, which the rest of the cast had already done before my arrival. What a schmuck.

It turned out to be a dream job because as a bad man, I got killed at the end of act one. Perfect, because I could then go swim in the beautiful pool that was part of the hotel/theatre. I swam, had fun, came back and was drying off and heard something that sounded very, very familiar. OMG, it was the finale number, and I was supposed to be in it. I rushed upstairs and snuck (yeah, right) to my partner, who was humorously glaring, and we finished the show.

Tom and I had a scene, as the only two on stage, where we plotted the demise of the good guy. The scene ends with us shaking hands. It seemed each night the pause before the blackout got longer as we stood holding hands. We mentioned it to the stage manager who told us she was in charge. The next night as we shook hands, I felt something in Tom's hand. I look down, while we stood in silence waiting for the lights to dim, and, hiding his hand from the audience, opens a box with an enormous 'diamond' ring. I look up and he mouths to me, "Will you marry me?" I could not help but smile, then snicker, as the lights finally faded to black. We got off and the stage manager, in a snit, came to us and told us how unprofessional we were. I told her not to be mad because we just got engaged and showed her my bauble. She scoffed and left. Went to the green room and showed off my engagement ring to the cast. We had a huge laugh. Oddly, the next night, as Tom and I shook hands, the stage went *immediately* black.

* * * * * * * * * * * * * * * * * * *

By now you know the only thing I know about "kars" and "komputers" is that they both start with the letter "K."

Summer. Got a 'new' car. One of my very favorites. A used, dark blue El Dorado in mint condition. Picked it up in Edmond, about a 25 minute drive home. A/C on and cruising along when suddenly my seat started getting warm. Odd. Kept going, as did the seat. It was getting really warm. Trying to drive and look around the control panel. Nada. Close to home and, how do I put this gently...my ass was on fire! Pulled in and called my incredible mechanic/friend Rick, who told me that I had a seat warmer that was turned on and told me how to turn it off. I loved that handy item on cold days. Miss it. However, I did learn, when it's really, really cold, to put a towel in the dryer just before leaving and my bottom is very happy. You might try it sometime. You're welcome.

I swear, when I see people tapping away at their phones texting, I am in awe. My fingers apparently have minds of their own. When Jan Garrett--wonderful, patient friend—talked me into getting a phone where I could text, I was ecstatic. Jan was at the Jewel Box and sent me a text. All excited, I typed back a reply. I swear, it took me like three minutes to type like three sentences. I hit send. Two seconds later I got a reply. Ugh! I was even happier when she helped me get a phone where you *talk* to text. Great invention. Speaking distinctly is imperative, obviously. I once was chatting and looked down, and it said something about "killing kids."

I feel sorry for those people with phones that don't allow cussing. It's my second language. As with all generations, what in the heck did we do before cell phones and carry- on computers? Like laughing at Grandpa telling stories of having to crank a car to get it going, or my grandmother watching the moon landing. What advances were made during her lifetime. Sometimes students would want me to tell stories about my youth as they laughed at the memory of walking two miles uphill in the snow to go to school, and the same uphill going home. Or something like that.

Humor!! It has gotten me through many potential disasters at school, the theatre, and life in general. For many people that is not something they can find. Two quotes I love about humor:

Audrey Hepburn: "I love people who make me laugh. I honestly think it's the thing I like most, to laugh. It cures a multitude of ills. It's probably the most important thing in a person."

Michelle Obama: "Get them to laugh and then they will listen."

Others:

"Laughter is the most inexpensive and most effective wonder drug. Laughter is a universal medicine."

"There is nothing in the world so irresistibly contagious as laughter and good humor."

"Laughter is a tranquilizer with no side effects, so please take regularly."

I think one of the hardest things for us humans to do is realize how unique we are and be proud of that. Oscar Wilde quote: "Be yourself. Everyone else is taken." We live our lives by what others think, many times never realizing what they say is trying to make us feel bad about ourselves, and sometimes for no reason.

One can pick almost any profession and say something bad about it, or the person doing it. I really find that appreciating what someone does that I can't do blows my mind. For example, open the hood of a car. It's a motor. One might think they would not do that job for whatever reason. A motor! The parts. The names. What it takes to make that puppy run. Let us see people for what they *can* do, and not what we think they *can't*. Tried to stay off of the soapbox, but that one has been a thorn in my side for many a year. Humor. Always a helper.

And one to remember, always, from the late Zig Ziglar: "Don't be distracted by criticism. Remember, the only taste of success some people get is to take a bite out of you."

As I took my last break and glanced back over my work, I decided to let my snippets fall where they may. I hope they're more fun to read that way, instead of traditional chapters. After all, I think I remember reading that whoever started People magazine, when asked why it uses short articles, commented that they wanted articles short enough to read in the crapper. If that's not true, what a hell of a story.

The End, Kaput, Auf Wiedersehen, Chop, chop lollipop, Adios, and Tha...Tha...That's all, Folks!

After this, I'm so hungry now, I think I'll go and make some liver and ...

OMG!

WRITER'S BLOCK!!

AUTHOR QUICKIE

(And I do mean quick)

CHARLES TWEED has written his one and only book.

ACKNOWLEDGEMENTS

Linda McDonald (Author/friend/mentor) who took the Herculean task of helping a newbie put together his snippets. Her generous comments about my writing and humor spurred me to do my best.

Jana Hester to whom I sent the first draft. For decades, she helped me with the written word at the Original Jewel Box Theatre with programs, press releases and *I before E except after C or when sounded like A.*

Jan Garrett who knows many of these snippets as well as myself, my having told them over and over to people who kept asking me to tell a certain story, and still laughing like she had never heard them before when she heard them again, or reading an early draft.

And, to everyone else, good or bad, happy or sad, who in some way or other was a part of my journey.

Made in the USA
Coppell, TX
12 January 2024

27626132R00085